Editor
Lorin E. Klistoff, M.A.

Managing Editor
Karen Goldfluss, M.S. Ed.

Editor-in-Chief
Sharon Coan, M.S. Ed.

Illustrator
Kathy Marlin

Cover Artist
Brenda DiAntonis

Art Director
CJae Froshay

Imaging
Ralph Olmedo, Jr.

Product Manager
Phil Garcia

Product Developer
Quack & Co.

Publishers
Rachelle Cracchiolo, M.S. Ed.
Mary Dupuy Smith, M.S. Ed.

Bible Stories From A to Z

Author

Mary Murray

Teacher Created Materials, Inc.
6421 Industry Way
Westminster, CA 92683
www.teachercreated.com

ISBN-0-7439-7102-7

©2002 Teacher Created Materials, Inc.
Reprinted, 2003
Made in U.S.A.

Table of Contents

Introduction

This book is a fantastic resource for parents, teachers, and Sunday school teachers! It is filled with a wonderful variety of Bible stories and exciting activities that accompany them.

Young children will have a marvelous time learning about Adam, Noah, Moses, Ruth, Esther, Jesus, Saul, and so many more Bible characters! After hearing each Bible story featured, the children will engage in such stimulating activities as making puppets, creating footprints with paint, constructing wind socks, connecting dots, using codes to color, completing mazes, and finding hidden pictures.

The book is divided into 26 mini-units, each featuring a letter of the alphabet. Each mini-unit contains the following reproducible components:

- A Bible story and questions for discussion
- A craft
- A prayer
- A snack idea
- A take-home story
- An alphabet page
- An activity page

The take-home stories are a wonderful way for children to share God's Word with their families. They also enable parents to discuss the Bible stories and characters with their children. If you wish, you can have the children create front and back covers for their books using construction paper, paint, markers, and other art supplies.

On page 143 is an Alphabet Quilt Recording Page. Make a copy of the quilt page for each child. Children will enjoy coloring in the squares of the quilt as they complete the lessons from A to Z.

Also, on page 144 is a blank journal page. Copies of the journal page can be used for such things as art projects, writing activities, parent newsletters, and classroom awards.

This book truly provides you with an easy way to help the children in your care learn all about God's Word in a fun and creative way!

A Adam in the Garden

Adam was the first person God created. God created Adam on the sixth day of creation—after He had created the land and seas, the sun, moon, stars, plants, trees, birds, fish, and animals.

Adam was very special to God. God loved him very much. God put Adam in a beautiful garden. Adam was very happy in the garden. God and Adam had a very special relationship.

God gave Adam several jobs. One was to take care of the garden. Another one was to give names to the animals God created.

God knew that Adam needed a helper and a friend. So God created the first woman. When Adam was asleep, God took one of Adam's ribs and used it to make Eve. Adam liked having Eve for a helper. He now had a new job to do—to help Eve obey God.

God commanded Adam and Eve not to eat fruit from the tree of knowledge of good and evil. One day, however, a serpent came along. It tricked Eve into eating the fruit from that tree. Adam ate some, too. Adam and Eve both disobeyed God. That is when sin first entered the world.

As a punishment, God sent Adam and Eve out of the beautiful garden. They had to go and live somewhere else. Adam and Eve started a family. They had two boys named Cain and Abel. Adam and Eve spent the rest of their lives learning more about God and how to obey Him.

Questions for Discussion

- Why do you think Adam was special to God?
- What were some of Adam's jobs?
- What happened when Adam and Eve disobeyed God?

A Adam in the Garden

 ## Arts and Crafts

Adam's Garden

Materials: large sheet of construction paper; construction paper scraps; pattern; scissors; glue or paste; 3" x 5" (8 cm x 13 cm) note card; other art supplies, such as tissue paper, pipe cleaners, yarn, dry pasta, buttons, or fabric scraps

Directions

1. Trace the pattern to the right on a note card and cut Adam out.

2. Use art supplies to create a beautiful garden scene on construction paper. Be sure to include all kinds of plants, trees, fruits, and vegetables.

3. Paste Adam on the construction paper.

4. Print *Adam's Garden* at the top of the paper.

5. Hang this picture up as a reminder to obey God.

 ## Snack Time

Frosted Animal Crackers

Ingredients: animal crackers, vanilla frosting, candy sprinkles

Provide the children with a handful of animal crackers. Have them identify each animal and then line the crackers up in a row on a piece of wax paper. Invite the children to dip the animal crackers halfway into the frosting, top with sprinkles, and let dry.

 ## Prayer

Pray this prayer or a prayer of your own asking God to help you learn to obey Him.

Dear God,

We praise you for creating Adam and Eve and all of mankind. Thank You for making each of us special. Lord, thank You that we can learn from the story of Adam in the garden. Help us to remember to obey You. You are a great God.

Amen.

A   Adam—The First Man

Color and cut out the pages. Staple them in order.

The First Man

1

Adam was the first person God created.   **2**

Adam lived in the Garden of Eden.   **3**

Adam named all the animals God created.   **4**

God created Eve to be Adam's helper.   **5**

God loves us!

God loved Adam and Eve very much.   **6**

A

Name _____

A Is for Adam

Trace and write.

Adam

A

Name _____

Adam Names the Animals

Color the picture of Adam and the animals. Cut out the words at the bottom of the page. Paste each word in the correct space on the page.

Baptism of Jesus

John the Baptist was Jesus' cousin. After John grew up, he lived in the desert. He wore clothes made of camel's hair. He ate locusts and wild honey. The Word of God came to John while he was in the desert. From that day on, John began to teach people. He told them to stop sinning. He told them to ask God's forgiveness. He told them to be baptized. John was preparing the way for Jesus to come. He baptized many people.

John taught people many good things. He told them to share with others. He said to only collect the amount of money they deserve. He told them not to take what wasn't theirs. He also told people to be thankful for what they had.

Some people thought John might be the Christ. But John told the people, "I am not the Messiah. Someone is coming who is greater than I. I baptize with water, but He will baptize you with the Holy Spirit."

One day, Jesus came to John. He asked John to baptize Him. John thought that Jesus should baptize him instead, but John obeyed Jesus and baptized Him. When Jesus came out of the water, heaven was opened. The Holy Spirit descended on Jesus like a dove. A voice came from heaven saying, " . . . *'You are my Son, whom I love; with you I am well pleased.'"* (Luke 3:22)

Questions for Discussion

- Who was Jesus' cousin?

- Where did John live?

- What did John eat?

- What did John say we should do?

- John said he baptized with water. What did he say Jesus baptized with?

- What kind of bird appeared above Jesus?

Baptism of Jesus

 Arts and Crafts

A Special Bird

Materials: dove pattern below, tagboard, scissors, hole punch, glue, string, white tissue paper, white feathers, pencil

Directions

1. Trace around the dove pattern on tagboard.
2. Cut out the pattern.
3. Cover the dove with lots of glue.
4. Wrap pieces of white tissue paper around the end of a pencil, and stick them to the glue.
5. Attach several feathers to the dove with glue.
6. Punch a hole and tie a string at the top of the dove.
7. Tell what God said when Jesus was baptized.

Dove Pattern

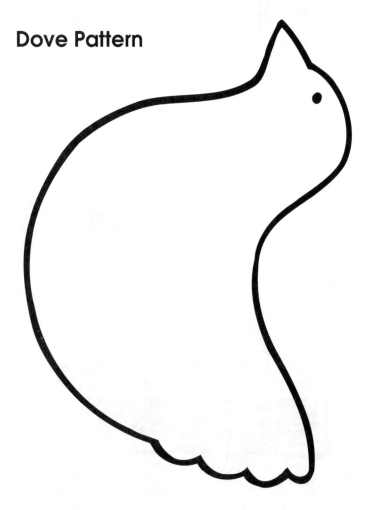

Prayer

Pray this prayer or a prayer of your own thanking God for baptism and the baptism of Jesus.

Dear Father,

Thank You for giving us the story of John baptizing Jesus. It's great how John the Baptist taught people to repent of their sin, believe in You, and be baptized. Thank You for showing us that Jesus is Your Son and that You baptized Him with the Holy Spirit. You are an awesome God. In Jesus' name I pray.

Amen.

Baptism of Jesus

 Snack Time

Honey Sticks

Ingredients: honey, pretzel rods

Provide each child with a pretzel rod and a small container of honey for dipping. (Small paper cups work great.) Invite the children to dip their pretzel into the honey and munch away as they talk about John the Baptist and how he ate locusts and honey.

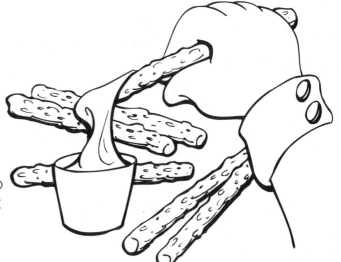

Color and cut out the pages. Staple them in order.

John the Baptist

John baptized men with water. **1**

John baptized women with water. **2**

John baptized Jesus with water. **3**

God baptized Jesus with the Holy Spirit. **4**

B Is for Baptism

Help Jesus find His way to John the Baptist so John can baptize Him. Color the picture.

START →

FINISH

Trace and write.

baptize

Name

A Terrific Teacher

John the Baptist taught people many things. John prepared the way for Jesus. Color the pictures. Cut and paste each shape in the matching space.

Creation

Long ago, there was no world, no sky, no planets, no animals, and no people. God created the world and all that is in it. He created everything in six days. On the seventh day, God rested. God is very powerful. He simply spoke words and things were created.

On the first day of creation, God said, "Let there be light," and there was light. On that day, He created day and night, light and darkness.

On the second day, God spoke, and He created the sky.

On the third day, God said, "Let dry ground appear. Let the land produce . . . plants and trees with fruit and seeds." And it was so.

On the fourth day, God created great lights in the sky—the sun, the moon, and the stars.

On the fifth day, God filled the waters with living creatures. He filled the skies with birds. So God created fish and lobsters, whales, eagles, robins and sparrows, and all other water creatures and birds.

Each day, God looked at all He had created. He liked it all. He said it was all good.

On the sixth day, God created all the different kinds of animals. He saw that it was good. On that same day, God created man. He said, ". . . *'Let us make man in our image . . . and let them rule over the fish of the sea, and the birds of the air, over the livestock, over all the earth, and over all the creatures that move along the ground.'"* (Genesis 1:26)

God created man in His own image. Then He made a woman. After God created the first man and the first woman, He saw all that He had made. He said it was very good.

On the seventh day, God finished his work. He rested. He blessed the seventh day. He set it apart as a very special day for Himself. God wants you to make one day each week special for Him, too.

Questions for Discussion

- What are some things God created?
- What did God say about everything He made?
- What did God do after He created everything?
- What day did God set apart for Himself?

14   ©Teacher Created Materials, Inc.

Creation

 Arts and Crafts

Creation Models

Materials: recyclable materials, such as cardboard tubes, empty juice and yogurt containers, spools, egg cartons, Styrofoam™; toothpicks; masking tape

Directions

1. Choose something from God's creation to create (a tree, animal, bird, fish, person, etc.) See examples below.
2. Construct your object using the materials available.
3. Display your creation on a table for all to see.

Creation

 Snack Time

Creation Salad

Ingredients: lettuce; fresh vegetables, such as broccoli, tomatoes, cucumbers, carrots, etc.; cheese; hard-boiled egg; salad dressing

Tear the lettuce into bite-sized pieces. Cut up a variety of fresh vegetables. Toss everything together in a bowl. Top the salad with cheese or slices of hard-boiled egg and salad dressing. Let the children enjoy a fresh salad with some of the vegetables that God created on the third day. While eating, have the children name some of their favorite fruits and vegetables.

 Prayer

Pray this prayer or a prayer of your own praising God for all the wonderful things He created.

Dear Lord,

We praise You for how powerful You are. It's amazing that You simply spoke, and everything was created! Thank You for making all the different animals in the world. Thank You for the plants and the trees, and for the sun, moon, and stars. Most of all, Lord, we thank You for creating people. You are a great God.

Amen.

Color and cut out the pages below and on page 17. Staple them in order.

1

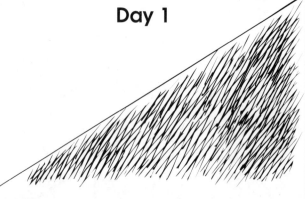

Day 1

God made light, day, and night. God said it was good. **2**

Creation

Day 2

God made the sky. God said it was good.

3

Day 3

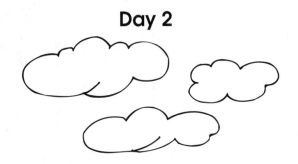

God made the land and seas, plants, and trees. God said it was good.

4

Day 4

God made the sun, the moon, and the stars. God said it was good.

5

Day 5

God made the birds and all the creatures of the sea. God said it was good.

6

Day 6

God made all the animals and man. God said it was very good.

7

Day 7

God rested.

8

C Is for Creation

Color the things God created.

Trace and write.

creation

C

Creation Quilt

Color the cards below. Cut them out. Practice putting them in the correct order.

Daniel in the Lions' Den

Daniel was a good man and a prophet from God. Daniel prayed to God three times every day.

King Darius gave Daniel a very important job. The king liked Daniel a lot.

Some evil men were jealous of Daniel. They made a plan to trick the king into making a new law that would get Daniel into trouble. The new law said: "You can't pray to any god except the king. If anyone does, he will be killed."

The king passed the law. But Daniel was brave. He still prayed only to God three times a day. Daniel trusted God.

When the evil men saw that Daniel still prayed to God, they told the king. The king liked Daniel. He didn't want to have him killed, but he knew that he had to follow his own law. So Daniel was taken to the lions' den and thrown in. The king said to Daniel, "I hope your God rescues you from the lions!"

That night, the king couldn't sleep. He was worried about Daniel. In the morning, the king ran to the den of lions and called out, "Daniel, was your God able to save you?" Daniel answered, "God sent his angel to shut the mouths of the lions. They haven't hurt me because God knows I have done no wrong."

The king had Daniel taken out of the lions' den and the evil men who got Daniel into trouble were thrown in.

After that, the king wrote a letter. He said that everyone must worship Daniel's God for He is the true God.

Questions for Discussion

- Who liked Daniel?
- What did the king give Daniel?
- Who tricked the king?
- What was the king's new law?
- How did God take care of Daniel?

D

Daniel in the Lions' Den

 Arts and Crafts

"Time to Pray" Pocket Clock

Materials: a metal lid from a frozen juice container (or a small aluminum pie plate), magnetic strip tape, scissors, permanent marker

Directions

1. Print the numbers 1–12 around the border of the lid for the clock face.
2. Cut two hands for the clock from the magnetic strip.
3. Move the hands on the clock, and make comments like these: "It's 3:00, snack time—time to pray!" "It's 8:00, bedtime—time to pray!"

 Snack Time

Roaring Good Rice Cakes

Ingredients: rice cakes; peanut butter or cream cheese; shredded cheese; small edibles, such as raisins, peanuts, or chocolate chips

Provide the children with the ingredients listed above. Have them spread the cream cheese or peanut butter onto their rice cakes. Then encourage the children to make a lion's face using the small edibles. They can add a lion's mane by gently pressing shredded cheese around the border of their rice cakes. The children can enjoy this roaring good snack as you talk about Daniel in the lions' den.

 Prayer

Pray this prayer or a prayer of your own asking God to help you be brave like Daniel.

Dear Heavenly Father,

Thank You so much for Daniel. We can learn how to be strong and courageous because of him. Thank You for listening to us each time we pray to You. Help us, Father, to become more like Daniel as we learn to walk in Your ways.

Amen.

Daniel

Color and cut out the pages. Staple them in order.

1

I can pray to God—just like Daniel.

2

I can love God—just like Daniel.

3

I can be brave—just like Daniel.

4

I can trust God—just like Daniel.

5

I can do all these things because God is always with me!

6

22

D

D Is for Daniel

Color the lions that contain letters that spell DANIEL.

Trace and write.

Daniel _____

Name _____

Time to Pray

You can pray many times each day—just like Daniel. Color the pictures. Cut out the clocks at the bottom of the page. Paste them in the matching boxes.

6:00

8:30

12:00

3:00

5:00

8:00

Elijah Fed by Ravens

Elijah was a prophet. God told Elijah things that would happen. One day, Elijah went to King Ahab. Elijah told him, "There will be no rain during the next few years unless I say so." And so it happened. There was no rain for a long time.

God was good. He took care of Elijah during the drought. God told Elijah to go to a special stream. Here God provided food and water for Elijah. Elijah drank from the stream, and God had ravens bring Elijah bread and meat every morning and every evening.

When the stream dried up, God told Elijah, "Go to the town of Zarephath. I have told a widow there to feed you." The widow was trying to prepare a meal. However, she only had a small amount of flour and oil—just enough to make one last meal. After that, she and her son would have nothing to eat and would die.

Elijah asked the woman for some water. He told her to make him a piece of bread. The woman said, "I have very little oil and flour—only enough for our last meal. Then my son and I will die." Elijah told the woman to do as he said and not to be afraid. He told her that she would have enough flour and oil until the Lord sent rain on the land.

The woman did as Elijah told her. She prepared bread from the flour and oil for Elijah. She also prepared a meal for her son and herself. There was still flour and oil left in her jars. God provided for the widow and her son. The flour and oil were not used up, just as Elijah had said.

After some time went by, the woman's son grew very sick. He died. The woman was very sad. She blamed Elijah for her son's death. But Elijah carried the boy upstairs and prayed aloud to the Lord. Elijah stretched out his body on top of the boy three times. He prayed, "Oh Lord, please let this boy live again." The Lord answered Elijah's prayer. The boy began breathing again.

Elijah carried the boy downstairs to his mother. She was very happy to see her son alive again. She said, "...'Now I know that you are a man of God and that the word of the Lord from your mouth is the truth.'" (1 Kings 17:24)

Questions for Discussion

- What did Elijah tell King Ahab?
- How did God take care of Elijah?
- In what ways does God take care of you?
- How did God take care of the widow and her son?
- How did Elijah help the widow's son?

E Elijah Fed by Ravens

 Arts and Crafts

Chalk on Sidewalk

Materials: colored, sidewalk chalk

Directions

1. Pair up with a friend.
2. Have your friend lay on the sidewalk or driveway. Trace around his or her body with the sidewalk chalk.
3. After you and your partner have been traced, draw or write ways that God provides for each of you on or near your own body print.
4. Add hair, face, and clothing to the drawings.

 Snack Time

Bird Skewers

Ingredients: small cubes of sausage or ham, small cubes of bread, toothpicks, bird stickers

Attach a bird sticker to a toothpick, and give one to each child. Invite the children to role-play the raven bringing bread and meat to Elijah as they use their own bird skewers to feed themselves snack.

 Prayer

Pray this prayer or a prayer of your own thanking God for providing you with food each day.

Dear Lord,

Thank You for giving us food each day—just like You did for Elijah and for the widow and her son. Thank You for the variety of foods You give us. Help us to be thankful for the food we have at each meal. You are a great Provider.

Amen.

Elijah

Color and cut out the pages. Staple them in order.

1

Elijah needed bread and water. God provided.

2

Elijah needed meat. God provided.

3

God provides for His people.

4

The widow needed oil and flour. God provided.

5

God provides for His people.

6

E

Name _____

E Is for Elijah

Find and circle the 5 hidden ravens  in the picture.

Trace and write.

Elijah _____

Elijah Pencil Practice

Color the pictures. Trace each line with your pencil.

F

Fish and Loaves

Jesus performed many miracles during His time on the earth. One of His well-known miracles is the miracle of the loaves and fish.

One day, Jesus crossed the Sea of Galilee with His disciples. Many people followed Him because they had seen the miracles He had performed. Jesus went and sat down with His disciples on the mountainside. He saw a great crowd of people coming toward Him. He soon began healing the sick.

When evening came, the disciples were ready to send the crowd away so they could get food. But Jesus knew what he was going to do.

One of the disciples had noticed a boy with five small loaves of bread and two fish. But surely that wasn't enough to feed all these people! About five thousand men had gathered by this time. Jesus took the five loaves and the two fish. He gave thanks. Then the disciples passed the bread and fish out to all the people. Everyone had enough to eat.

When everyone was done eating, Jesus asked His disciples to gather the food that was left over. The disciples gathered enough to fill twelve baskets.

After Jesus performed this great miracle, many more people believed in Him.

Questions for Discussion

- How many loaves of bread did the boy have?
- How many fish did the boy have?
- How many baskets of leftover food did the disciples gather?
- Jesus provided food for many people. How does God provide your family with food?

Fish and Loaves

 Arts and Crafts

Fish and Loaves

Materials: one 12" x 18" (30 cm x 46 cm) sheet of colored construction paper, one fish shape and one loaf shape cut from a sponge (See patterns on page 32.), shallow pans of tempera paint, multi-colored glitter, black marker

Directions

1. Fold down the two corners of the paper as shown, so that they meet together in the middle and leave a border along the bottom.

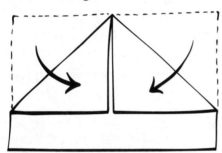

2. Dip the sponges in the paint. Make five loaf prints and two fish prints along the bottom of the paper.

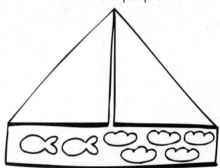

3. Use the marker to print **Jesus performed a miracle!** on the flaps of the paper, as shown.

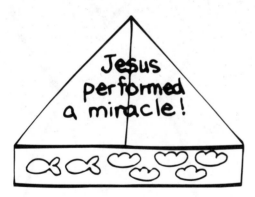

4. Underneath the flaps, make many prints of fish and loaves. Then sprinkle glitter on the wet prints (multi-colored glitter on the fish, gold glitter on the loaves).

5. Let dry.
6. Retell the story to a friend or a family member. Be sure to lift the flaps of the page when saying, "Jesus performed a miracle!" Then show all the sparkly fish and loaves.

Fish and Loaves

 Snack Time

Roaring Good Rice Cakes

Ingredients: fish-shaped crackers, pretzel nuggets, sesame sticks, or other loaf-shaped crackers

Give each child a paper cup. Have the children count two fish and five loaves into their "baskets." Then announce, "Jesus performed a miracle!" Invite the children to fill their "baskets" to the top with fish and loaves.

Children will enjoy munching their snack and retelling the story of the miracle of loaves and fishes.

 Prayer

Pray this prayer or a prayer of your own praising Jesus for how great He is.

Dear Jesus,

You are a mighty God. Thank You for all the miracles You performed while You were on the earth. Help us to remember that You are still powerful today. Thank You for loving us and for showing us Your great power.

Amen.

Fish and Loaf Patterns

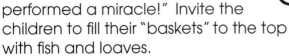

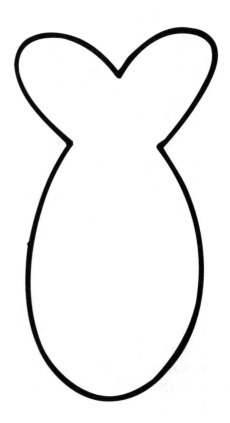

Fish and Loaves

Color and cut out the pages. Staple them in order.

Miracle of Loaves and Fish

A small boy had two fish. **1**

A small boy had five loaves of bread. **2**

There were lots of people. They were hungry. So Jesus performed a miracle. **3**

Everyone ate lots of fish. **4**

Everyone ate lots of bread. **5**

The people were no longer hungry because Jesus performed a miracle. **6**

F

Name

F Is for Fish

Color the 5 loaves of bread that are the same. Color the 2 fish that are the same.

Trace and write.

Fish Puzzles Word Cards

Color the fish. Cut them out. Cut each fish on the dashed lines. Store the fish in an envelope. Use the fish puzzles to practice reading words. Use the words to help you retell the story of the miracle of the loaves and fish.

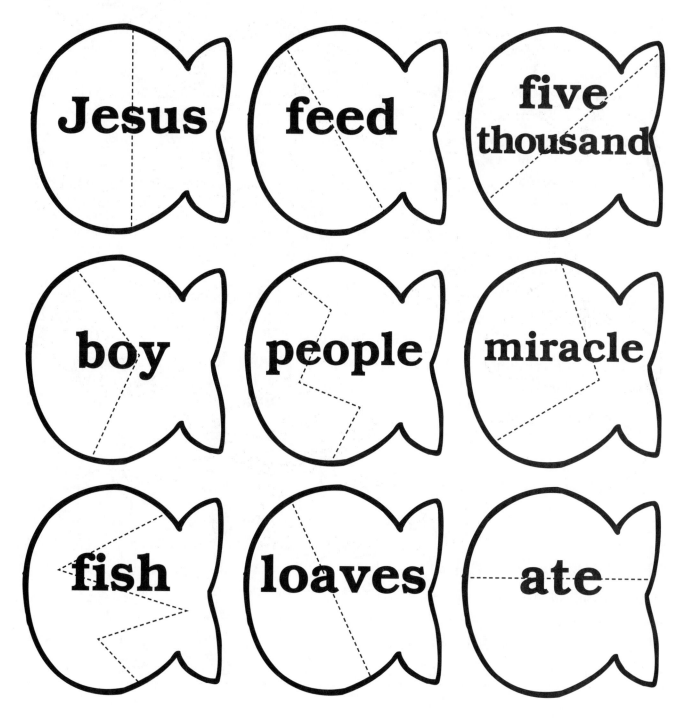

Goliath and David

The Israelites and the Philistines were enemies. One of the Philistines was a very tall man. They said he was a giant because he was nine feet tall! He was a very strong man. His name was Goliath.

Goliath wanted to fight any man from the Israelite army that would agree to fight him. Goliath said, "If I win the fight, you will be our slaves. If any Israelite wins the fight, we will be your slaves."

But no one wanted to fight Goliath, for he was very big and very strong.

David was a shepherd boy. He went to visit his brothers in the Israelite army. He heard Goliath's challenge. He asked King Saul if he could fight Goliath. The king said, "David, you are small, and he is big. He is strong, and you are very young. You cannot fight him."

David replied, "While tending my father's sheep, I have fought a bear, and I have fought a lion. If I can fight off those two animals, I can fight this giant."

The king replied, "If you must go, then take my armor and my sword with you. And may the Lord be with you."

So David put on the armor and took the sword. But he was not used to wearing armor, so he took it off.

"I will fight him without the armor," David said. So he took his shepherd's stick and his sling. He found five smooth stones from a nearby stream, put them in his bag, and went to meet the giant Goliath.

When Goliath saw David, he was angry, because David was just a small, young man. The giant shouted at David, "*Come here . . . and I'll give your flesh to the birds of the air and the beasts of the field!*" (1 Samuel 17:44)

David said to the Philistine, "You come against me with sword and spear, but I come against you in the name of the Lord. The Lord will help me beat you." Then David took a stone from his bag and put it in the sling. He struck Goliath in the forehead and killed him.

David got his strength and power from the Lord. He beat Goliath. David grew up to become one of the greatest kings of the Israelite nation.

Questions for Discussion

- Why didn't anyone want to fight Goliath?
- Why was David so brave?
- How did the Lord help David win the fight?
- What has God helped you do?

Goliath and David

Arts and Crafts

David's Pouch of Stones

Materials: 12" (30 cm) squares of fabric; pieces of twine or yarn; 5 smooth, round stones (real or cut from tagboard); permanent markers

Directions

1. Use the markers to decorate one side of each stone with a colorful design.
2. Write (or dictate) each of the following words on a stone: **The battle is the Lord's.**
3. Place 5 stones in the center of the fabric.
4. Gather up the corners and tie the bundle with the twine or yarn.
5. Use this to tell others the story of David and Goliath.

 ## Snack Time

Giant–Sized Sandwich

Ingredients: large loaf of French bread, a variety of meats and cheese, lettuce, tomato, and other sandwich toppings

Invite the children to help you prepare this giant-sized sandwich. Cut the loaf of bread down the center. Invite the children to fill the sandwich with meat, cheese, and toppings. Cut the sandwich into child-size portions and enjoy together.

 ## Prayer

Pray this prayer or a prayer of your own asking God to help you trust in Him like David did.

Dear God,

Help us to become more like David—strong and courageous. Help us to know that You are with us and that "the battle belongs to You." Thank You for giving us strength and power, just like You did for David.

Amen.

G

Goliath and David

Color and cut out the pages. Staple them in order.

David and Goliath

Goliath was big.
He was a warrior. **1**

David was small.
He was a shepherd. **2**

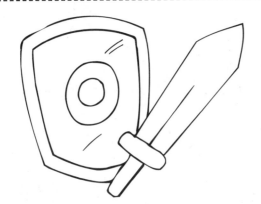

Goliath fought with armor
and a sword. **3**

David used a stone and
a sling. **4**

David said, "The battle
belongs to the Lord." **5**

Goliath lost. David won. **6**

G

Name _____

G Is for Goliath

Connect the dots to draw Goliath. Color the picture.

Trace and write.

Goliath _____

_____

Name _____

Measuring Goliath and David

Use the ruler here to measure how tall David and Goliath are. Then use other things in the room to measure them.

How tall in:	David	Goliath
inches	_____	_____
paper clips	_____	_____
buttons	_____	_____
crayons	_____	_____

Healings of Jesus

As Jesus walked along, He saw a man who had been blind since the day he was born. Jesus spit on the ground. He made some mud with His spit and dirt. Jesus put the mud on the man's eyes. He told the man, "Go and wash in the pool of Siloam." The man did exactly as Jesus said, and he was able to see! He was very happy and very thankful that Jesus healed him.

Jesus healed the man from blindness so that people would see the work of God and believe that He is the Light of the World.

Many of the people in town saw the man. They were surprised that he could see. They asked him, "How were your eyes opened?" The man explained, "Jesus made some mud. He put it on my eyes. Then told me to go wash in the pool of Siloam. I went and washed, and then I could see."

Jesus had healed the blind man on the Sabbath day. No one was supposed to do any work on the Sabbath day. Some men called Pharisees were not happy with Jesus. They didn't think He should perform a miracle on the Sabbath day. The Pharisees were also angry at the man. They kicked him out of the synagogue.

Jesus heard about this. He went to the man and asked him, "... 'Do you believe in the Son of Man?'" (John 9:35) He replied, "Who is he? Can you tell me so that I can believe in Him." Jesus said, "You have seen Him. He is the one you are speaking with."

Then the man said, "I believe, Lord." And he worshipped Jesus.

Questions for Discussion

- What did Jesus do to heal the blind man?

- Did the blind man believe that Jesus was the Son of God?

- Why were the Pharisees mad at Jesus?

- What other miracles of healing did Jesus do?

Healings of Jesus

Jesus Pattern

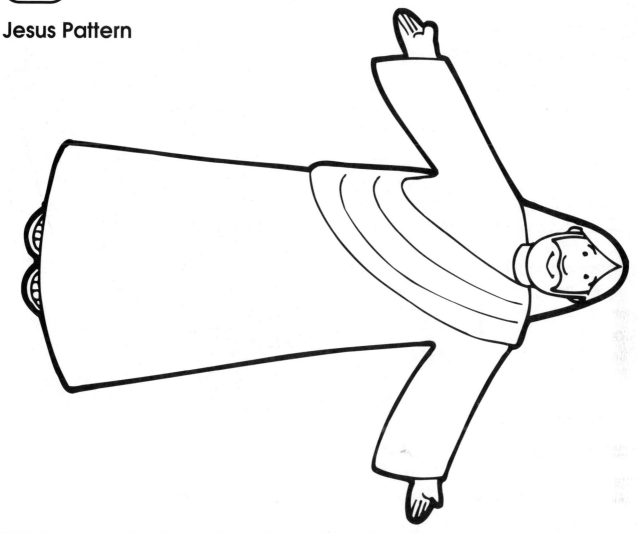

Color and cut out the pages below and on page 44. Staple them in order.

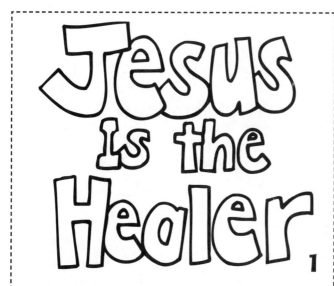

1

I can see!

Long ago and far away, Jesus healed a blind man. **2**

Name _____

H Is for Healer

Use the code to color the picture.

15-yellow   16-brown   17-green   18-blue

Trace and write.

Healer

Jesus Heals

Color the pictures. Cut out each picture at the bottom of the page and paste it in the matching space to show Jesus heals.

Before	After
leper	
crippled	

Before	After
blind	
bleeding	

Israelites

God spoke to Abram. He told Abram to leave his country and his people and go to a land that God would show him. God said he would bless Abram and make his name great. All the people on the earth would be blessed through Abram. This was the beginning of a new nation called Israel. This new nation would become God's special, chosen people. They would be called Israelites.

So when Abram was 75 years old, he and his wife, Sarai, left his country and did as the Lord told him. They set out for the land of Canaan.

When they arrived in Canaan, the Lord appeared to Abram. He said, "Abram, you are going to have a son. Look at the heavens, and count the stars in the sky. Your descendants will be as many as the stars in the sky." Even though Abram was old and his wife was much too old to have children, Abram believed God. God knew this. He knew that Abram was a righteous man.

When Sarai heard that she was to have a son, she laughed. She never thought she could have a baby when she was 90 years old! But the Lord was faithful. Sarai gave birth to a son just as the Lord said. They named him Isaac, which means "he laughs."

God later gave Abram the name Abraham, and Sarai was to be called Sarah. God was faithful to Abraham and Sarah. Through Abraham, the new nation of Israel began. They were God's chosen people. They were the ones who were freed from slavery, wandered in the desert for 40 years, and then entered the Promised Land.

Abraham was a very special man. He is called the Father of all Nations. Some of the people born from Abraham's line are Isaac, Jacob (Israel), Joseph, Judah, Boaz, Obed, Jesse, David, Joseph (Jesus' father on the earth), and Jesus. (Luke 3:23–34)

Questions for Discussion

- What was the name of God's chosen people?
- What did Abram name his son?
- Why did Sarai laugh when God said she would have a son?
- Who are some of the special people that were related to Abraham?

Israelites

 Arts and Crafts

"God Is Faithful" Footprint Art

Materials: a brown grocery bag; large, shallow pan of tempera paint; dish pan of soapy water; towels; markers; glitter pens, glitter glue, or other art supplies

Directions

1. Cut along the side and then cut out the bottom of the grocery bag so that you have a long strip of brown paper.

2. At the top of the paper, print the following: **We are thankful to God. He is faithful to us.**

3. Take off your shoes, step into the pan of paint, and walk across the paper, making a pattern of footprints.

4. Then step into a bucket of soapy water to wash your feet.

5. Once the artwork is dry, trace around each footprint with a marker, glitter glue, glitter pens, or other art supplies.

6. Hang this as a reminder of the Israelites wandering in the desert and how God is faithful to the people He loves.

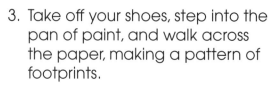

Israelites

 Snack Time

Desert Trail Mix

Ingredients: chocolate candies, pretzels, snack crackers, raisins, peanuts

Combine two or three cups each of the above snack foods into a large bowl. Mix well. Scoop into bags. Provide each child with a bag of trail mix. Have a walking snack time. Take the children on a walk outdoors. Stop and munch the trail mix at several points along the way to give the children an idea of how the Israelites wandered in the desert.

 Prayer

Pray this prayer or a prayer of your own thanking God for watching over you and for providing for your wants and needs.

Dear Heavenly Father,

Thank You for taking care of the Israelites in all the different ways You did. We also thank You for watching over us. Thank You for leading us with Your Word. Thank You for giving us the things we need and so many things we want. You are a mighty God. We love You and praise Your name.

Amen.

Color and cut out the pages below and on page 50. Staple them in order.

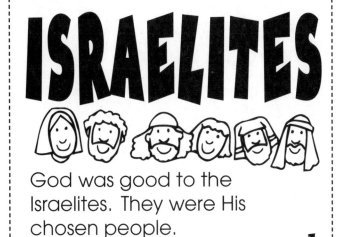

God was good to the Israelites. They were His chosen people.

1

He freed them from slavery in Egypt.

2

Israelites

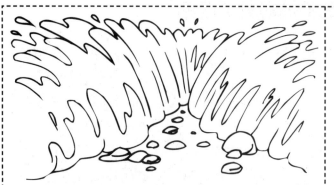

He parted the Red Sea so they could walk across on dry ground.

3

God was good to the Israelites. They were His chosen people.

4

God gave the Israelites water to drink when they were thirsty.

5

He fed them with manna and quail each day.

6

The Israelites wandered for 40 years, and their sandals never wore out.

7

God was good to the Israelites. They were His chosen people.

8

50

I

Name _____

I Is for Israelites

Find and circle 6 hidden stars ⭐ in the picture.

Trace and write.

Israelites _____

Name _____

God's Chosen People

Cut out Abraham and Sarah's family tree below and paste it to a piece of construction paper. Then cut out the picture cards. Match them to the correct face.

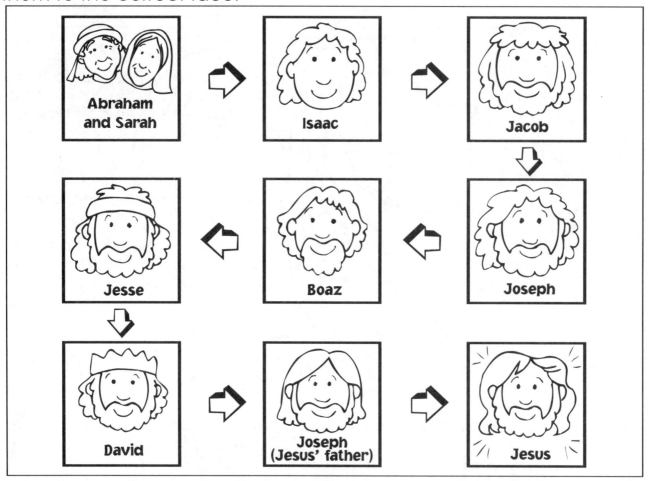

Abraham and Sarah → Isaac → Jacob

Jesse ← Boaz ← Joseph

David → Joseph (Jesus' father) → Jesus

Joseph   Isaac   Jesse   Jacob

David   Boaz   Jesus   Joseph (Jesus' father)

Joseph's Story

Jacob had 12 sons. He loved his son Joseph most of all. Jacob gave Joseph a beautiful coat. Joseph's brothers were jealous. They were also jealous because Joseph could interpret dreams.

One day, while the brothers were out tending sheep, they saw Joseph coming. They plotted to kill Joseph. When Joseph arrived, they took off his special coat. They threw him into a deep pit. Later, the brothers dipped Joseph's coat in goat's blood. They told their father that a wild animal had eaten him. Joseph's father was very sad.

Then some traveling merchants came by. The brothers decided to sell Joseph as a slave to the men.

The merchants took Joseph to Egypt. There Joseph worked hard for Potiphar, one of Pharaoh's officials. For a while, Joseph was put in jail for something he didn't do. He got out of jail by telling Pharaoh what his dream meant. Pharaoh put Joseph in charge of all of Egypt.

A great famine came to Egypt, but Joseph had saved a lot of food for Egypt. One day, some men came to Joseph to buy food. It was Joseph's brothers! Joseph recognized his brothers, but they did not recognize Joseph. Joseph gave them food. He told them who he was.

The brothers were sorry for what they had done to Joseph. Joseph forgave them. He got to see his father. His family all went to live in Egypt. God had worked everything out for good.

Questions for Discussion

- Why were Joseph's brothers jealous of him?
- What did the brothers do to harm Joseph?
- What did God do to help Joseph?
- Joseph forgave his brothers. Tell about the last time you were forgiven.

Joseph's Story

 Arts and Crafts

Joseph's Special Coat

Materials: brown grocery bags; scissors; crayons and markers; art supplies, such as fabric scraps, ribbon, yarn, buttons, beads, sequins; construction paper; glue

Directions

1. Cut down the center of one side of the bag.
2. Cut a neck hole and two armholes as shown.
3. Use the materials to decorate a special coat.
4. Go outside or parade through the building so others can see your beautiful coat.

 Snack Time

Cookies of Many Colors

Ingredients: unfrosted sugar cookies, frosting, colored sugars or sprinkles

Provide each child with a cookie. Invite the children to spread frosting on top of their cookies and then top with colorful sprinkles and sugars.

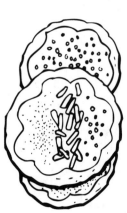

Have the children walk around the room and look at each other's colorful cookies before they eat them. Remind the children how Joseph's father gave him a special coat of many colors.

Prayer

Pray this prayer or a prayer of your own telling God that you trust Him.

Dear Father,

We love You very much. Thank You for teaching us about trusting You in the story of Joseph. We can see that You were working in his life even when things weren't going the way he wanted them. Thank You, Father, that we know that You are always working in our lives, too, and that everything that happens is allowed by You.

Amen.

54

Joseph's Story

Color and cut out the pages. Staple them in order.

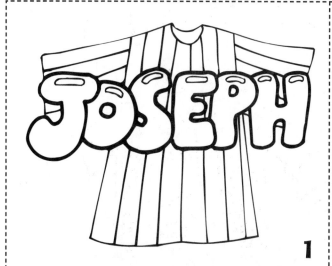

1

Jacob had 12 sons. Joseph was his favorite son.

2

Jacob gave Joseph a special coat. Joseph could interpret dreams.

3

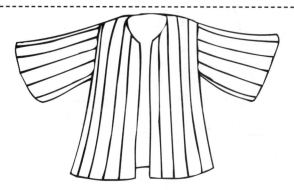

Joseph's brothers were jealous. They threw Joseph in a pit and sold him as a slave.

4

God helped Joseph. He was put in charge of all the land of Egypt.

5

Everything worked out God's way.

6

J Is for Joseph

Use the code to color the picture.

△ = yellow   ▢ = blue   ○ = orange   ☆ = green

Trace and write.

Joseph _____

Joseph's Coat of Many Colors

Joseph had 11 brothers. Color each brother's coat a different color.
Number each coat from 1 to 12. Color Joseph's coat.

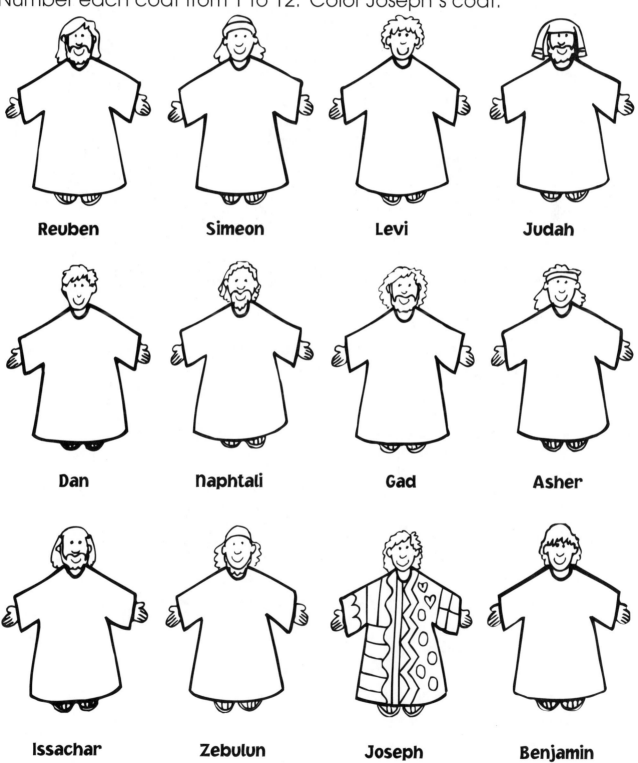

Reuben   **Simeon**   **Levi**   **Judah**

Dan   **Naphtali**   **Gad**   **Asher**

Issachar   **Zebulun**   **Joseph**   **Benjamin**

King David

Saul was the first king of the Israelite nation. Samuel, the prophet, had anointed him as the king. Saul had won many battles against the enemies of God's people. But God wasn't happy with Saul as king, because he disobeyed His commands.

Samuel went to Saul. He said, "Since you have disobeyed the Lord's commands, God does not want you as king."

God told Samuel to go to Bethlehem to find a man named Jesse. God said he had chosen one of Jesse's sons to be the next king.

So Samuel went to Bethlehem to see Jesse and his sons. Samuel

looked at the oldest son. He thought he looked like he would be a good king, but the Lord said, "I do not look at the outward appearance of a man. I look at his heart. This is not the son that will be king."

Then Jesse called his next son and had him pass in front of Samuel. He was not the one the Lord had chosen either. Seven of Jesse's sons passed before Samuel, but not one of them was chosen by God.

Samuel asked, "Are these all the sons you have?" Jesse said, "No, there is still the youngest son, David. He is out tending sheep." Samuel sent someone to get David. When David came in, Samuel could see that he was very strong and healthy. When David arrived, the Lord said to Samuel, "This is the one. Anoint him as king." So Samuel took the oil and anointed David in front of his brothers. Immediately, the Spirit of the Lord was with David.

Later, David would fight and kill Goliath, the giant Philistine. He would also grow up to become Israel's greatest king. And Jesus would be born into David's family many years later!

As king, David wrote many of the Psalms. God loved David.

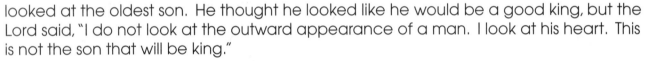

Questions for Discussion

- Why didn't God want Saul to be king any longer?

- What are some of the great things King David did that make him special?

- Joseph forgave his brothers, tell about the last time you were forgiven?

- Would you make a good king or queen?

King David

 Arts and Crafts

King's Castle Art

Materials: large amount of 1" (2.54 cm) gray paper squares; a sheet of blue construction paper; markers; glue; scissors; brown construction paper; red felt or paper; castle pattern on page 60 for tracing

Directions

1. Trace the castle onto the sheet of blue construction paper.
2. Glue the gray squares onto the castle to represent bricks.
3. Draw a flagpole and then cut a flag from red felt. Glue it to the pole.
4. Cut a 2" x 4" (5 cm x 10 cm) drawbridge from brown construction paper. Fold the end and glue it to the castle as shown.

 Snack Time

King's Crown Sandwich Stacks

Ingredients: slices of sausages, cheese, round crackers, olive halves

Invite the children to stack the food in the following order from the top to bottom as they make their King's Crown: cracker, sausage, cheese. Top it off with an olive half and enjoy.

 Prayer

Pray this prayer or a prayer of your own praising God for King David and thanking Him for what we can learn from David's life and the book of Psalms.

Dear God,

Thank You for putting the story of David in the Bible. Help us to become like him. Help us to love You and try to please You as he did. Thank You, God, for the Psalms that David wrote. They teach us a lot about praising You and trusting in You.

Amen.

King David

Castle Pattern

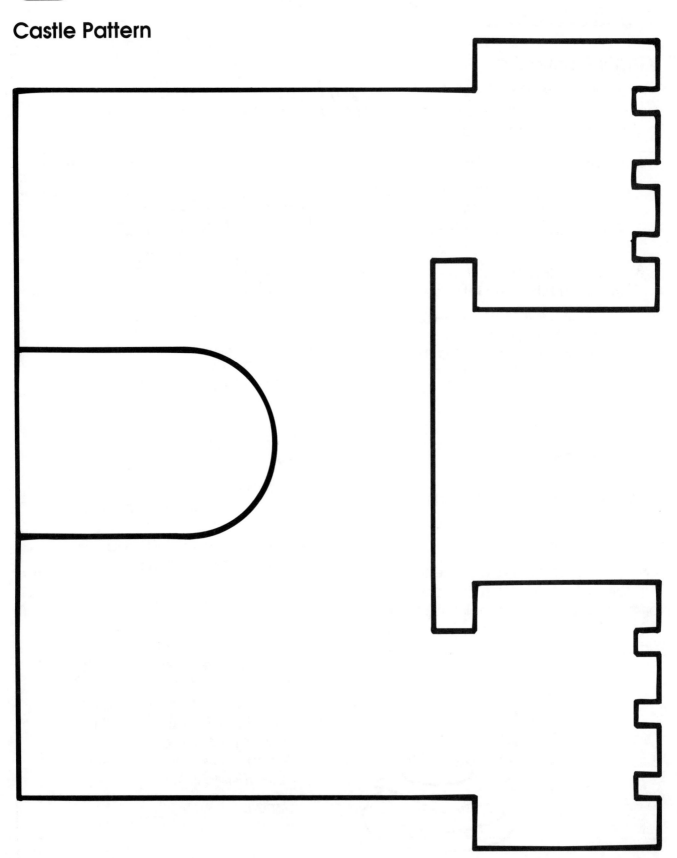

King David

Color and cut out the pages. Staple them in order.

David was anointed as
Israel's next king.

1

He beat Goliath with a
stone and sling.

2

He fought and won many
battles.

3

He sinned, and he repented.

4

He wrote many of the
Psalms.

5

You can be like David and
make God happy, too.

6

K

Name _____

K Is for King David

Help Samuel find David to make him king.

START

FINISH

Trace and write.

king

King David Game Board

Find one coin and two game markers. Put the markers at START. Toss the coin. When you land on a star, move ahead one space. Talk about the different events in David's life as you move across the board. The first one to the FINISH wins.

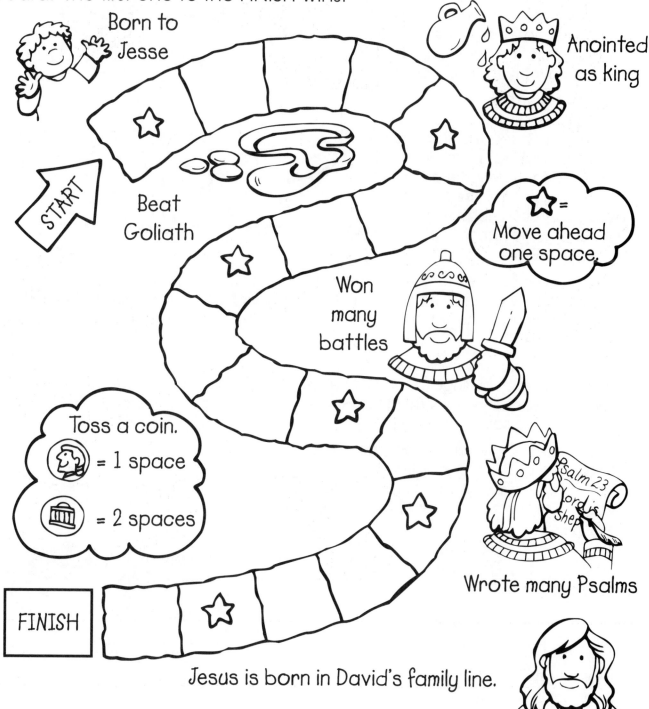

Born to Jesse

Anointed as king

Beat Goliath

☆ = Move ahead one space.

Won many battles

Toss a coin.
= 1 space
= 2 spaces

Wrote many Psalms

FINISH

Jesus is born in David's family line.

Lost Son

Jesus told this parable. A man had two sons. The youngest son asked his father for his share of the family money. Then this son took all of his money and moved to another city. While in this city, the son spent all of his money. He lived a very sinful life. Some time later, a severe famine came to the land. The young son had no money left. He had no food. He was hungry. He found a job feeding pigs for another man. The son was so hungry that he wanted to eat the pig's food.

The son began to realize how wrong he had been. He knew he had sinned against God and his father. So he decided to walk home and ask his father to forgive him. The son thought maybe he could at least work as a hired hand for his father. Then he would have food to eat.

The son began walking home. When he was still a great distance off, the father saw his son coming along the road. The father was so happy! He knew that his son had done wrong, but he was ready to forgive him. He praised God that his son had returned home.

The father told his servants, "Go and bring the best robe for my youngest son to wear. Put a ring on his finger. Give him new sandals for his feet." He also told the servants to prepare the best meal for his son. "We're going to celebrate. My son has come home," he said.

The older son saw all that was going on. He became angry. He was jealous that his father was giving a celebration for his younger brother. But the father said to him, "My son, you are always with me. Everything I have is yours. We have to celebrate because your brother was dead, but now he is alive again; he was lost and now is found."

Questions for Discussion

- What did the young son do?
- Why did he want to come home again?
- Why was the older brother jealous?
- Have you ever had to forgive someone? Tell about it.
- Tell about a time when someone forgave you.

L

Lost Son

 Arts and Crafts

Rejoice Piñata

Materials: white paper lunch bag, white tissue paper, colored markers, large amount of 1" (2.54 cm) colored tissue paper squares, glue, pencils, large amount of small candies, yarn

Directions

1. Print **Rejoice** on one side of the bag. Use markers to add designs all over the bag.
2. Wrap each tissue square around the end of a pencil. Dip it in glue, and attach it to the bag near the word **Rejoice** (as shown).
3. Let the piñata dry.
4. Put candy pieces and crumbled pieces of tissue paper in the bag.
5. Tie the piñata shut with a piece of yarn.
6. The next time a family member repents of a sin or admits doing wrong and apologizes, the family can have a celebration and break the piñata open.

 Snack Time

Forgiving Hearts Biscuits

Ingredients: refrigerator biscuits, cinnamon sugar

Give each child a piece of biscuit dough. Let them shape their biscuit pieces into heart shapes. Have the children dip their biscuit pieces into cinnamon sugar. Bake as directed. Serve warm. Top with butter.

 Prayer

Pray this prayer or a prayer of your own asking God to help you love others.

Dear Lord,

Thank You for the Parable of the Lost Son. Sometimes it's hard to love people who do things that are wrong. Help us to love those people, especially when they say they are sorry for what they have done. Thank You, Father, for forgiving us when we sin, just like the father in the story.

Amen.

Lost Son

Color and cut out the pages. Staple them in order.

The Lost Son

A man had two sons. The youngest son asked his dad for money.

1

The youngest son left home. He lived a sinful life.

2

Let me help you, Dad!

The oldest son stayed home. He helped his dad.

3

The youngest son soon realized he was wrong. He asked his father to forgive him. And he did.

4

The father gave a party for his youngest son. The oldest son was jealous.

5

The father said to the oldest son, "You are always with me. Everything I have is yours. Let's celebrate today because your brother was lost, but now he is found."

6

L Is for Lost Son

Help the lost son find his way home.

Trace and write.

lost son

Name _____

Lost Son Stick Puppets

Color and cut out the stick puppets. Tape a craft stick to the back of each picture. Use the puppets to tell the Parable of the Lost Son.

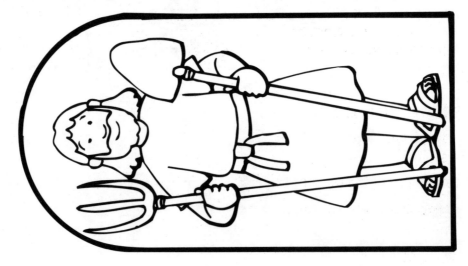

Bible Lesson (Exodus 2:1–10)

Moses' Life

The Israelites were forced to become slaves in Egypt. They were under the rule of Pharaoh. Pharaoh didn't want them to have more children because he was afraid that soon there would be too many Israelites. So Pharaoh made a new law. The law said that any Israelite baby boy was to be killed.

One Israelite woman had just given birth to a son. She knew that her son was very special, and she loved him very much. This mother wasn't going to let Pharaoh kill her son. So she hid him for three months. Then she thought of a plan. She made a basket from reeds. She covered it with tar so that no water could get inside. The mother placed her son inside the basket and set it in the river.

The baby's sister was named Miriam. Miriam watched as the basket floated away. Soon Pharaoh's daughter saw the basket in the river. When she looked inside, she saw the baby crying. She wanted to keep the baby. Miriam saw what happened, so she went up to the princess and said, "Would you like me to go and find a woman that will nurse the baby for you?"

The princess said, "Yes."

Miriam went and got her mother, who nursed him and raised him until he got older. Then she took him back to Pharaoh's daughter. The princess named the boy Moses.

Moses grew up in Pharaoh's home. Later on, Moses was chosen by God to deliver His people from slavery in Egypt.

Questions for Discussion

- Why did Pharaoh want to kill all the Israelite boys?

- How did the mother save her son?

- What did Moses do when he grew up?

M

Moses' Life

 Arts and Crafts

Baby Moses

Materials: modeling clay or dough, blue construction paper

Directions

1. Use the modeling clay to form a basket (as shown).
2. Make baby Moses out of the clay. Set the baby inside the basket.
3. Cut a strip of blue paper to represent the river.
4. Retell the story of baby Moses, using the materials.

 Snack Time

M Is for Moses

Ingredients: M&M's® chocolate candies, napkins, graham crackers, frosting

Give each child five candies. Have the children shake the candies in their hands and let them fall onto the napkin. For each *M* that is facing up, have the children tell one thing they know about Moses. For each *M* facing down, have them tell another word from the Bible that starts with the letter *M*.

Afterwards, let each child put frosting on a graham cracker. Give them more M&Ms so they can use the candies to form the letter *M* on their graham crackers.

 Prayer

Pray this prayer or a prayer of your own praising God for the story of Moses.

Dear Father,

Thank You for putting the story of Moses in the Bible. It's wonderful how You saved Moses. Thank You for working things out so that Moses could do what You wanted him to do when he grew up. Help us to remember this story and to know that You have a perfect plan for our lives, too.

Amen.

Moses' Life

Color and cut out the pages. Staple them in order.

MOSES

Pharaoh wanted to kill all the Israelite baby boys. **1**

Moses' mother hid him in a basket in the river. **2**

God saved Moses. **3**

Moses grew up in Pharaoh's house. **4**

God had a special plan for Moses' life. **5**

God has a special plan for your life, too. **6**

M Is for Moses

Find the word **MOSES** 5 times in the puzzle. Color each one a different color.

F	Z	B	M	G	M
V	L	M	O	A	O
W	M	O	S	E	S
M	O	S	E	S	E
Y	Q	E	S	Y	S
J	D	S	T	R	C

Trace and write.

Moses

M

Name _____

A Hairy Story

Color and cut out Moses and the sentence strips. Paste each sentence strip in a space on Moses' beard. Cut along the dashed lines on Moses' beard. Wrap each strip around a pencil to make Moses' beard curl.

1. Moses was special to God.

2. God spoke to Moses from a burning bush.

3. Moses delivered the Israelites from slavery in Egypt.

4. God gave Moses the Ten Commandments.

5. Moses wrote the first five books in the Bible.

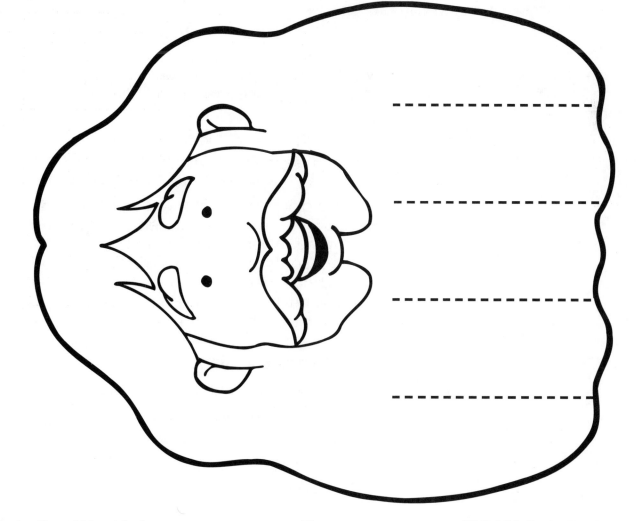

Noah and the Ark

Many years after God created the earth, the people became very wicked. God did not like that. It made Him very sad.

There was one good man. His name was Noah. Noah was a righteous man, and he obeyed God. He lived with his wife. They had three sons. Their names were Shem, Ham, and Japheth.

God decided that He no longer wanted all the evil people on His earth. So He decided to send a great flood. The flood would be so big that all the people would be destroyed. But God wanted to save Noah because he was a good man. God told Noah to build a very large ark. He told him exactly how big to make it and what materials to use. Noah did exactly as God commanded him.

Then God told Noah to take two of every living creature onto the ark. He did. Then Noah, his wife, and his three sons and their wives also got into the ark, just as God commanded him.

Then it started raining. It rained for 40 days and 40 nights. Noah and his wife and his sons and their wives and all the animals were safe inside the ark when God flooded the earth. Every other living thing on the earth was destroyed by the floodwaters.

God didn't forget about Noah. He sent a great wind over the earth. The waters went down, and the land dried. When Noah reached dry ground, he praised God. Noah built an altar, made a sacrifice to God, and then worshipped Him. God sent a rainbow on that day, and He promised never to send a flood to destroy the earth again.

Questions for Discussion

- Why did God want to flood the earth?
- Why did God save Noah?
- Who else did God save with Noah?
- What did Noah do after the flood?

Noah and the Ark

 ## Arts and Crafts

Painting Rainbows

Materials: large sheets of poster board; red, orange, yellow, green, blue, indigo, and purple tempera paints; paintbrushes; art shirt; string; hole punch; scissors

Directions

1. Draw an arch across the sheet of posterboard.
2. Paint a rainbow with the colors in order as listed above.
3. After it dries, cut out the rainbow shape.
4. Punch one or two holes in the top and then tie a string through the holes for hanging.
5. Hang it up as a reminder of God's faithfulness to Noah and to us.

(Note: You may need to demonstrate painting for this project.)

Snack Time

Fruit Rainbow

Ingredients: a variety of fresh or canned fruits

Clean, peel, and cut up a variety of fresh or canned fruits. Have the children help you arrange the fruits, forming a large rainbow on the tray. After everyone admires the rainbow for a short time, invite the children to take several pieces of fruit from the rainbow and make their own mini rainbows on a small paper plate. Then have children eat the fruit as they remember God's promise to Noah.

 ## Prayer

Pray this prayer or a prayer of your own asking God to help us obey Him.

Dear God,

Thank You for the story of Noah. He was a good example to us of what it means to obey You and do exactly what You ask of us. Thank You for Your Word that teaches us how to obey You. Help us remember Your promise to Noah every time we see a beautiful rainbow in the sky.

Amen.

Noah and the Ark

Color and cut out the pages. Staple them in order.

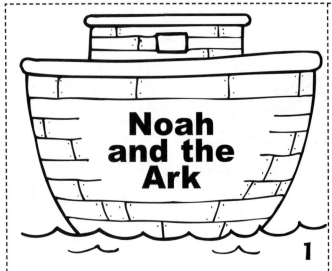

God told Noah to build a big ark. Noah did what God told him to do. **2**

God said, "Bring two of every animal into the ark." Noah did what God told him to do. **3**

God saved Noah and his family because Noah did what God told him to do. **4**

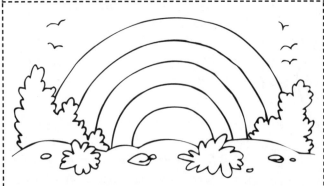

God loved Noah very much because he did what God told him to do. **5**

Noah praised God. **6**

N

N Name _____

N Is for Noah

Color the picture.

Trace and write.

Noah _____

Name _____

Noah's Ark Story Cards

Cut out the word cards at the bottom of the page. Paste them in order on the ark. Color the picture.

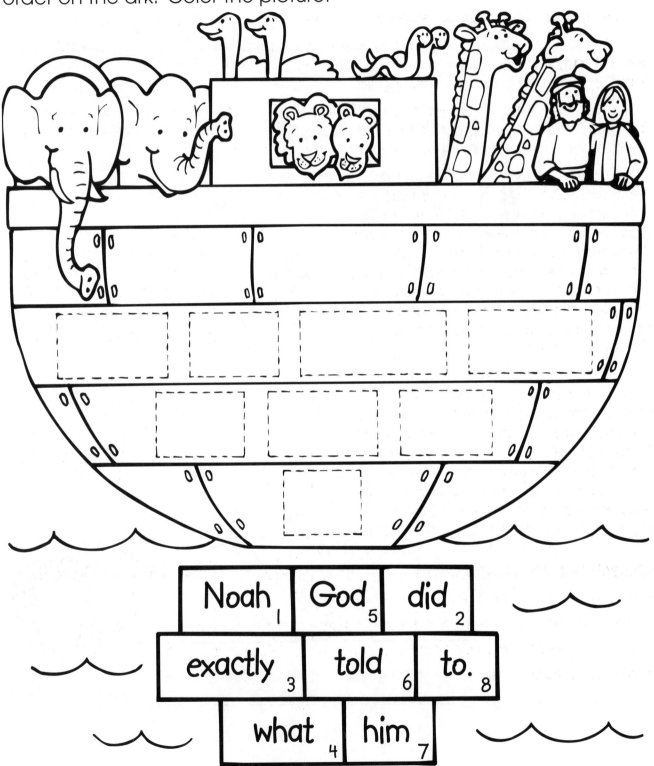

Noah ₁ God ₅ did ₂

exactly ₃ told ₆ to. ₈

what ₄ him ₇

One and Only Son

One day, an angel named Gabriel came to Mary and said, "Greetings! God loves you very much. He is with you." Mary was a little frightened and confused. The angel said, "Do not be afraid, Mary. God has chosen you for something special. You will give birth to a son. You are to name Him Jesus. He will be called the Son of the Most High. His kingdom will never end."

Mary said, "I am the Lord's servant. I will do whatever He wants."

Months later, Mary had the baby. Her husband was Joseph. She named the baby Jesus. Many people came to worship Him for He was the Savior of the world—the Messiah that they had been waiting for.

Jesus grew into a boy and then into a man. He lived a life just like other people. But Jesus never sinned, because He was God. Jesus spent much of His life performing miracles and teaching people to repent of their sins and believe in Him.

Many people didn't believe that Jesus was God's Son. They got angry with Him and wanted to kill Him. Some people had Him nailed to a cross. It was there that Jesus died. Many people were sad when Jesus died, especially his mother, Mary, and His close friends and disciples. But Jesus knew that He would rise from the dead and go back to His Father in heaven.

After Jesus was dead for three days, He rose from the grave. He came back to the earth and spoke with many people. Later, He ascended into heaven to be with His Father. Many people were standing nearby when this happened. They watched as Jesus rose into heaven. Jesus promised that He would come back again to rule the earth some day.

Questions for Discussion

• Who is Jesus' true Father?

• Who was Jesus' mother on the earth?

• What did Jesus teach people about?

• Why did people want to kill Jesus?

One and Only Son

 Arts and Crafts

Jesus Flags

Materials: plastic straw or pencil, colored construction paper, scissors, paste or glue, magazine or newspaper

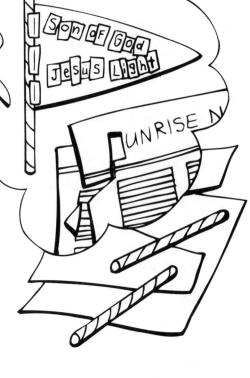

Directions

1. Make a list of names for Jesus that are mentioned in the Bible. Some examples include the following: King of Kings, Lord, Savior, Light, Bread of Life, Master, Messiah, Redeemer, Deliverer, Christ, Wonderful Counselor, Almighty God, Son of God, Son of Man, etc.

2. Talk about what each name means.

3. Cut a flag shape from the construction paper. Tape it to the straw or pencil as shown.

4. Cut out letters from a magazine or newspaper to spell out one of the various names for Jesus. Glue it on one side of the flag.

5. Put a different name on the other side of the flag.

Snack Time

O Necklaces

Ingredients: O-shaped cereal, such as Cheerios™ or Fruit Loops™

Invite the children to count and string cereal pieces onto a piece of yarn or string. (Suggestion: Children can count out 27 pieces of cereal to represent the 27 books of the New Testament that teach us about Jesus.)

Children can name the books of the Bible or different names for Jesus as they eat their necklaces for a snack.

One and Only Son

 **Prayer**

Pray this prayer or a prayer of your own thanking God for Jesus, His one and only Son.

Dear God in Heaven,

Thank You so much for giving us Your Son, Jesus. You loved Him so much, and yet You sent Him to the earth to live and die and become our Savior. We thank You, Jesus, for all You have done for us. You are the King of Kings and Lord of Lords. Help us to follow You.

Amen.

Color and cut out the pages. Staple them in order.

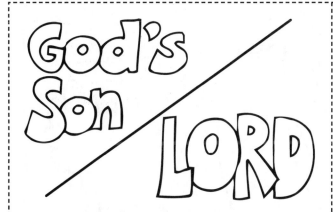

Jesus is God's only Son.
Jesus is the Lord. **1**

He was born in Bethlehem.
He is the Living Word. **2**

He came to live on the earth.
Jesus never sinned. **3**

Jesus died for me,
and He will come again. **4**

Name _____

O Is for One and Only Son

Color the picture.

Trace and write.

only son

Name _____

Jesus Panorama

Color the pictures. Cut out the pieces following the solid lines. Fold the panorama pieces on the dashed lines. Paste the matching letters together.

Jesus the One and Only

He was born in a manger. | He grew in wisdom.

A

He healed people.
He taught people. | Thank you, Jesus.
He performed miracles.

A | B

He died on the cross. | He rose from the grave.

B

Paul in Prison

Paul and Silas were followers of Jesus. After Jesus died and rose into heaven, Paul and Silas went around telling other people about Jesus.

Many people did not want to hear about Jesus. In fact, many people got very angry with Paul and Silas for talking about Jesus.

Some people in the town of Philippi took Paul and Silas, beat them up, and threw them into prison. In the prison, they had to wear chains.

Paul and Silas didn't like being in prison, but they knew that Jesus was their Savior. They knew that God loved them and that He would take care of them.

One night around midnight, Paul and Silas began praying and singing hymns to God. Other people in prison were listening to them praise the Lord. Suddenly, there was a violent earthquake, and the foundations of the prison were shaken. God performed a great miracle. All the prison doors flew open, and every prisoner's chains came loose.

The jailer who was guarding the men saw the prison doors open. He didn't know what had happened. He was frightened. He thought that he would be in trouble if the prisoners escaped. But Paul spoke to the guard. He told him that everything was alright and that all the prisoners were still there. The guard realized that Paul was a man of God. He asked Paul, "What must I do to be saved?" Paul said, ". . . 'Believe in the Lord, and you will be saved.'" (Acts 16:31)

Paul and Silas taught the prison guard and his family some things from God's Word. The man took care of Paul and Silas. He became friends with them. He and his whole family believed in the Lord on that day. They were filled with great joy because they, too, had come to believe in Jesus, the Son of God.

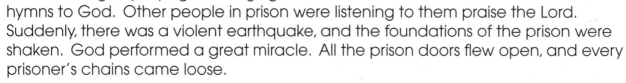

Questions for Discussion

- Why did people put Paul and Silas in prison?
- What happened when Paul and Silas praised God?
- Why did Paul and Silas still praise God, even when they were in prison?
- What did the jailer do?

Paul in Prison

 Arts and Crafts

Praise Sticks

Materials: cardboard tubes, two 4" (10 cm) squares of contact paper, two 2" (5 cm) squares of paper, popcorn kernels, stickers, markers, streamers or yarn, tape

Directions

1. Decorate each tube with stickers or markers.
2. Hold a 2" square of paper on one end of the tube. Then wrap a square of contact paper over it to secure the end shut (as shown).
3. Pour $\frac{1}{8}$ cup (30 mL) of popcorn kernels into the tube.
4. Cover the other end of the tube with the remaining paper square and contact paper square.
5. Tape several streamers or stands of yarn to one end of the tube.
6. Use the Praise Stick to make a joyful noise as you sing a favorite praise song to Jesus.

 Snack Time

Raisin Praisin' Snack

Ingredients: various sizes and shapes of whole grain and/or sweet cereal pieces, raisins, other dried fruits

Have the children combine all the ingredients together in a large bowl and mix. The children can then sit in a circle as you pass out cups of this snack. Invite the children to take turns praising God for things He's done in their lives as they enjoy the treat together.

P

Paul in Prison

 Prayer

Pray this prayer or a prayer of your own telling God that you know He is powerful.

Dear God,

Thank You for the story of Paul and Silas in jail. We can see how mighty and powerful You are. Lord, we know that You are still mighty and powerful today. Thank You that Paul and Silas still praised You, even when they were in prison. Help us to praise You every day, too.

Amen.

Color and cut out the pages. Staple them in order.

Paul was in prison, but he still praised the Lord.

1

I praise you, Lord.

Paul was in chains, but he still praised the Lord.

2

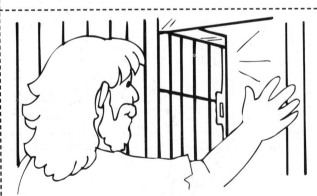

God heard Paul's praise, and He opened the prison doors.

3

When do you praise the Lord?

4

P

Name _____

P Is for Paul

Find and circle the letters in **PAUL** in the picture.

We Will praise God!

Trace and write.

Paul _____   _____

P

Name _____

Praise God

Cut on the dashed lines. Color the page. Fold on the dotted lines.
Write words of praise to God inside.

Quail from Heaven

The Israelites had been slaves in Egypt for many years. God helped Moses free the Israelites from slavery. The Israelites were on their way to the Promised Land. They had been walking in the desert for many days, and they were very hungry. God was leading the people in a pillar of clouds by day and a pillar of fire by night.

When God's people were first freed from slavery, they were very happy. But soon, they forgot how good God was. They began to complain because they were hungry. Some of them said, "We would rather have stayed in Egypt as slaves than starve to death out here in the desert." God heard the Israelites complaining. He said to Moses, "I will rain down bread from heaven for you. The people are to gather enough food to eat each day."

God did as He promised. Each morning when the Israelites awoke, the ground was covered with manna, bread from heaven. It was like a wafer sweetened with honey. The people ate all they wanted.

But the Israelites weren't satisfied. They complained some more. They wanted meat. So God sent quail for the people to eat. Each evening, quail flew into the camp. The people ate as much quail as they wanted. God gave the Israelites what they wanted.

God's people ate manna for the next 40 years. God told Moses to have the people save some of the manna in a jar and keep it as a reminder of how God provided for His people in the desert.

Later, when the Israelites entered the Promised Land of Canaan, they would be able to settle down and grow their own food.

God always provides what His people need.

Questions for Discussion

- Who led the Israelites out of slavery in Egypt?
- Why did they become unhappy?
- What did God give the Israelites to eat?
- How long did the people eat manna?

Quail from Heaven

 Arts and Crafts

Quail Everywhere

Materials: one sheet of construction paper, shallow tray of paint, feathers, black markers

Directions

1. Print **Quail Everywhere** across the top of the paper.
2. Dip your hands into the paint. Cover the page with handprints.
3. Once the prints are dry, draw eyes, a beak, and feet on each quail.
4. Glue one or more feathers to each quail.
5. Let dry.

 Snack Time

Quail Salad on Crackers

Ingredients: small chunks of boneless, cooked chicken; mayonnaise; salt; pepper; crackers; paprika

Mix the chicken with the mayonnaise. Add salt and pepper to taste. Spread the mixture on crackers. Top with paprika and enjoy.

Invite the children to think of different ways we prepare and eat chicken. Then brainstorm ways the Israelites may have prepared their quail meat.

Prayer

Pray this prayer or a prayer of your own thanking God for giving what you need.

Dear Lord,

You are a great God. Thank You for giving us so many things. You provide us with everything we need, just like the Israelites. Thank You for caring for us and loving us so much.

Amen.

Quail From Heaven

Color and cut out the pages. Staple them in order.

1

The Israelites wanted meat. **2**

They'd had enough manna to eat. **3**

In the evening, God sent quail. **4**

God sent lots and lots of quail. **5**

God provided for His people. **6**

Q

Name _____

Q Is for Quail

Color only the .

Trace and write.

quail

92

Quail in a Nest

Fold and crumble the sides of a brown lunch bag down to form a nest. Write or draw what you are thankful for on the quail, color them lightly, and cut them out. Set them in the nest.

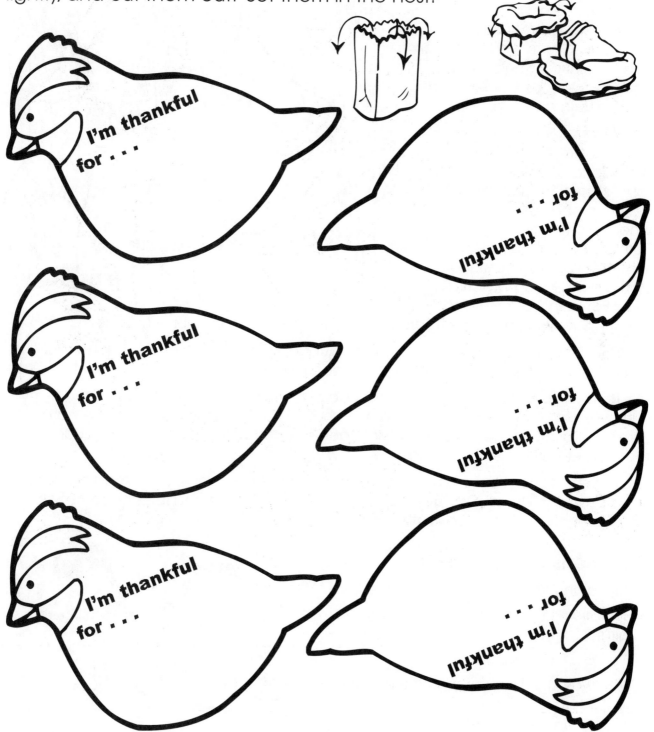

I'm thankful for . . .

I'm thankful for . . .

I'm thankful for . . .

I'm thankful for . . .

I'm thankful for . . .

I'm thankful for . . .

Ruth Is Faithful

Ruth is a very special woman. She has a book in the Bible named after her. It tells about her life story.

Naomi was married to Elimelech. They moved to Moab during a time of great famine when there wasn't much food to be found. Naomi and Elimelech had two sons. Elimelech died, and the two sons married women named Ruth and Orpah.

Years later, Naomi's sons died. So Naomi was left without a husband and without her two sons. Naomi thought it would be best to go back to Bethlehem where she was from. Naomi told Ruth and Orpah to stay in Moab with their own mothers and to start a new life. So Orpah did just that. But Ruth was faithful to Naomi. She wouldn't let her mother-in-law travel back to Bethlehem alone.

Ruth and Naomi traveled to Bethlehem together. In Bethlehem, it was harvest time for barley. Ruth gathered barley in the fields for their food.

Ruth worked in a field that belonged to a man named Boaz. Boaz noticed that Ruth was new to the area. He heard how she had been faithful to Naomi by staying with her. Boaz watched over Ruth. He made sure she was able to gather enough food. Later, he and Ruth married.

Ruth and Boaz had a son named Obed. Obed had a son and named him Jesse. Jesse's son was David. David is the boy who fought Goliath and later became a great king. Through the line of David, the Lord Jesus Christ would someday be born.

Questions for Discussion

- Why didn't Ruth's family have much food?
- How did Ruth show her mother-in-law she was faithful to her?
- Who did Ruth marry?
- Who was later born through the line of Ruth and Boaz?

Ruth Is Faithful

 Arts and Crafts

Ruth Puppet

Materials: one 12" x 12" (30 cm x 30 cm) square of white tissue paper, one 12" x 12" (30 cm x 30 cm) square of colored tissue paper, tissue, yarn, black marker, glue

Directions

1. Crumble a tissue into a ball.
2. Wrap the white tissue paper square around the ball (as shown).

3. Lay the colored tissue paper square over the white, leaving a space for Ruth's face (as shown).
4. Tie with a piece of yarn.

5. Dip the end of the pencil in glue and insert the pencil into the head.

6. Use the marker to draw Ruth's face.
7. Use the puppet to tell the story of Ruth.

 Snack Time

Barley Bundles

Ingredients: pretzel sticks, licorice string or bread twist ties

Remind the children how Ruth gathered stalks of barley from the field. Invite the children to make their own little bundle of barley stalks for snack time. Have each child count out 10 pretzel sticks and then tie them together in a bundle with a piece of string licorice or a bread twist tie.

 Prayer

Pray this prayer or a prayer of your own asking God to help you grow in your love for your family.

Dear Father in Heaven,

Thank You for Ruth. Help us find ways to show love for the people in our families. Help us to be faithful to our families and to honor our fathers and mothers. Thank You for the blessing of a family.

Amen.

Ruth Is Faithful

Color and cut out the pages. Staple them in order.

1

Ruth was faithful. You can be faithful, too.

2

Ruth helped her family. You can help your family, too.

3

Ruth cared about others. You can care about others, too.

4

God blessed Ruth.

5

God will bless you, too.

6

Name

R Is for Ruth

Color the picture.

Trace and write.

Ruth

Name _____

I Can Be Faithful, Too!

Cut the top corners off a brown lunch bag to form a house, as shown. Decorate the house to look like your home. Color the pictures below. Write or draw pictures telling how you can show people in your family that you are faithful to them and to God. Add more pages if you like. Cut them out and place the pages inside your home to remind you to be faithful.

Saul's Big Change

After Jesus died and went to heaven, many people didn't like Christians who believed in Him. Saul was one of those men. He hated people who believed in Jesus. In fact, he thought it was good when other people killed Christians.

One day, something very strange and miraculous happened to Saul. He was on his way to Damascus to find people who believed in Jesus Christ and take them as prisoners. While he was walking, a light from heaven flashed around him. He fell to the ground. He heard a voice say, "Saul, Saul, why do you persecute Me?"

Saul asked, "Who are you, Lord?" The voice answered, "I am Jesus, whom you are persecuting. Get up and go into the city. There you will be told what to do."

The men traveling with Saul didn't know what to do. They heard the sounds but didn't see anything. When Saul got up from the ground, he opened his eyes, but he couldn't see. He was blind.

Saul's friends led him by the hand into Damascus. For three days, Saul was blind. He didn't eat or drink anything.

In Damascus, the Lord called a man named Ananias. In a vision, the Lord told him to go lay his hands on Saul and give him back his sight. Ananias was a Christian. He didn't want to go near Saul. He knew that Saul hated people who believed in Jesus.

God told Ananias to go anyway. So Ananias went to the house where Saul was staying. He laid his hands on Saul. He said, "The Lord Jesus who appeared to you on the road has sent me so that you may see again and be filled with the Holy Spirit."

Right then, something like scales fell from Saul's eyes, and he could see again. Saul got up. He was baptized. Then he spent several days with Jesus' disciples in Damascus. Saul believed in Jesus, and now he was a Christian, too. Soon Saul began preaching in the synagogues that Jesus is the Son of God.

Many people couldn't believe how Saul had changed. Saul, who later became known as Paul, grew more and more powerful. He kept telling others that Jesus is the Christ.

Questions for Discussion

- Where was Saul going when the miracle happened on the road?
- What did Jesus do to Saul?
- What happened after Ananias spoke with Saul and touched him?
- How did Saul change?

Saul's Big Change

 Arts and Crafts

"Follow Jesus" Wind Sock

Materials: 9" x 12" (23 cm x 30 cm) sheet of construction paper, markers, crepe paper streamers, tape, hole punch, yarn, curling ribbon

Directions

1. Print **I will follow Jesus!** on the construction paper.
2. Decorate the paper with markers.
3. Roll the paper onto a tube, and tape it together at the seam.
4. Punch two holes at the top. Tie a string through the holes.
5. Cut several 12" (30 cm) streamers from crepe paper. Tape them along the bottom of the wind sock.
6. Cut several strands of curling ribbon. Attach them to the bottom of the wind sock.
7. Hang up the wind sock.

 **Snack Time**

"No Peeking" Vegetable and Fruit Fun

Ingredients: a variety of fresh vegetables and fruits, vegetable dip or fruit dip

Have the children work with a partner for this snack time activity. Invite the children to gather two pieces of each type of vegetable and fruit and place them on a paper plate. Have one child in each pair close his or her eyes, while the partner hands him or her a vegetable or fruit piece to touch, smell, and taste. The children will enjoy guessing which vegetable or fruit they have without looking. After both children in each pair have tried each type of food, provide the children with more vegetables and fruit, as well as vegetable dip or fruit dip to enjoy with their healthy snack.

Saul's Big Change

 **Prayer**

Pray this prayer or a prayer of your own thanking God for helping Saul and others to understand God's love.

Dear Father,

Thank You so much for the story of Saul on the road to Damascus. It's wonderful how You helped him believe in Jesus. Thank You for helping us believe in Jesus, too. Help us Father, to be more like Saul and to teach others about Your love.

Amen.

Color and cut out the pages. Staple them in order.

Saul was walking down a road. A bright light flashed around him.

1

Why do you persecute Me?

It was Jesus. He spoke to Saul. He made Saul blind.

2

Saul went to Damascus. Ananias helped him see again.

3

Saul became a believer in Jesus—just like you and me.

4

Name _____

S Is for Saul

Color the picture.

Trace and write.

Saul _____

Footprint Fun

Color the picture. Write on each footprint ways you can follow Jesus. Cut out the footprints and the picture. Glue them on another sheet of paper. Tell someone how you are following Jesus.

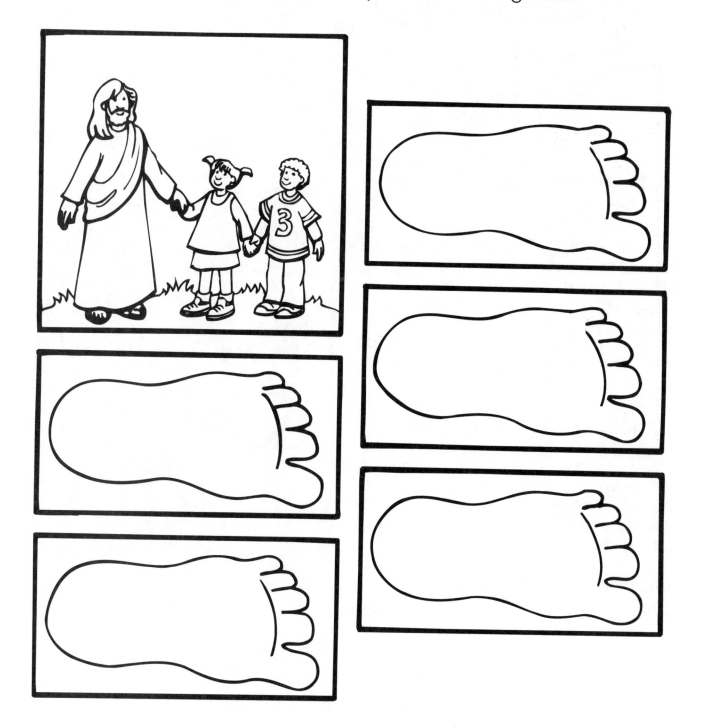

Ten Commandments

God helped Moses free the Israelites from slavery in Egypt. They were going to the Promised Land. After they had been traveling for about three months, God spoke to Moses. He told Moses that He would come to the people in a dense cloud. The people would hear Him speaking. They would put their trust in Moses.

God loved His people. He wanted them to be good and holy people. So He prepared for them a set of commandments to follow. God told Moses to gather all the people at the foot of the mountain. The people gathered, but they were frightened. They had never heard God speak before. God said if the people touched the mountain they would be killed. God told Moses to come up the mountain. Moses went. God told Moses 10 rules that the people were to follow to show their love for God. He wrote them on two stone tables. Moses was on the mountain for forty days. The people got tired of waiting for him to come down. So they made a golden calf and worshiped it instead of the one true God.

When Moses came down from the mountain, He saw the people dancing, singing, and worshipping the golden calf. Moses was very angry. He threw down the stone tablets, and they broke into pieces. Many people were punished or killed for worshipping the golden calf.

God wrote the Ten Commandments a second time on two stone tablets. Then Moses took the tablets to the people. He read them God's commandments: Love God with all your heart; worship only God; keep God's name holy; keep the Lord's day special. These first four commandments taught the people how to show love for God.

The next six commandments taught the people how to show love for each other: Obey your father and mother; do not kill; be faithful in marriage; do not steal; do not lie; do not be jealous of what others have. The people heard all God's commands. They promised to obey the Lord.

Questions for Discussion

- Why were the people afraid to hear God speak?
- What did the people do while Moses was up on the mountain with God?
- Why did Moses break the stone tablets?
- What are some of the rules God gave the people to follow?

Ten Commandments

 Arts and Crafts

1 to 10 Counting Jar

Materials: plastic container or jar with a lid (or resealable baggie); large amount of small objects, such as beans, pennies, seeds, candies, dry pasta, shells, beads, colorful snips of yarn

Directions

1. Count out sets of objects from one to 10— one peanut, two seeds, three pennies, etc. Place all the materials in a jar.
2. Open the jar. Spill out the contents.
3. Sort the objects into groups. Count each set.
4. Arrange the sets as shown on the left, from one to 10.
5. Recite the Ten Commandments when you are finished working with the materials.

🥄 **Snack Time**

Number Writing

Ingredients: dry, flavored gelatin powder; gelatin with fruit in it

Have the children wash their hands. Sprinkle about 1/8 (30 mL) cup of gelatin powder onto a plastic lid. Give one to each child. Invite the children to gently shake the lid to cover it with the powder. Have the children form the numbers one to 10 in the powder with their fingers as you instruct them. Allow the children to lick their finger between numerals. Encourage them to name or recite the Ten Commandments as they write their numbers.

After this tasty writing activity, give the children a bowl of prepared gelatin and fruit to eat.

Ten Commandments

 Prayer

Pray this prayer or a prayer of your own asking God to help you obey His commands.

Dear Lord,

Thank You for the Bible that teaches how You want us to live. Help us, Father, to obey the Ten Commandments that You gave to Moses and the Israelites. Help us also to obey the other things You tell us in Your Word.

Amen.

Color and cut out the pages below and on page 107. Staple them in order.

The Ten Commandments

1

God gave us 10 rules to obey. We can follow them and walk in God's way.

2

Ten Commandments

1. Love God with all your heart.
2. Worship only God.

3

3. Keep God's name holy.
4. Keep the Lord's day special.

4

5. Always obey your mom and your dad.
6. Do not kill.

5

7. Be faithful in marriage.
8. Do not steal.

6

9. Do not tell a lie.
10. Do not be jealous of what other people have.

7

God gave us 10 rules to obey. We can follow them and walk in God's way.

8

T

T Is for Ten Commandments

Color the picture.

The Ten
1. Love God with all your heart.
2. Worship only God.
3. Keep God's name holy.
4. Keep the Lord's day special.
5. Always obey your mom and dad.

Commandments
6. Do not kill.
7. Be faithful in marriage.
8. Do not steal.
9. Do not tell a lie.
10. Do not be jealous of what others have.

Trace and write.

ten

Ten Commandments Number Match

Practice matching each commandment to its number words. Cut out the cards below and glue on a sheet of construction paper.

1. Love God with all your heart.	2. Worship only God.	3. Keep God's name holy.
4. Keep the Lord's day special.	5. Always obey your mom and dad.	6. Do not kill.
7. Be faithful in marriage.	8. Do not steal.	9. Do not tell a lie.	10. Do not be jealous of what others have.

one	two	three	four

five	six	seven

eight	nine	ten

Upper Room

It was Passover time. The Jewish people celebrated this holiday every year. They would remember how God was faithful to them and how He freed them from slavery in Egypt.

Jesus and His disciples were going to celebrate the Passover, too. Jesus knew that He was going to die soon.

His disciples asked Him, "Lord, where should we go to prepare the Passover meal?" Jesus said, "Go into the city. A man there will show you an upper room. That is where we will celebrate the Passover meal together." (This is also called the Last Supper, because it's the last meal that Jesus ate with His disciples before He died.)

When the men entered the city, they found the upper room. Everything for the meal was prepared.

It was in this room that Jesus washed the feet of His disciples. As He washed their feet, He told them to love one another and to serve one another.

Also in this upper room, Jesus broke bread. He gave thanks to His Father, and said, "Take this and eat. This is my body." Jesus then shared the cup of wine with His disciples. They ate and drank together for the last time. Jesus wanted His disciples to remember Him whenever they ate or drank.

During the meal, Jesus also said that one of His disciples would betray him. This disciple would turn Him over to be crucified. The disciples wondered who would do that to Jesus. It was Judas Iscariot.

Questions for Discussion

- What were Jesus and His disciples celebrating?
- What were some things that happened in the upper room that day?
- What did one of the disciples do to Jesus?
- Who was that disciple?

Upper Room

✏️ **Arts and Crafts**

Upper Room Diorama

Materials: small box or shoe box, construction paper, glue, scissors, washcloth, a smooth round stone, permanent marker, patterns on page 112

Directions

1. Set the box on its side.
2. Draw and cut out objects from construction paper that may have been found in the upper room (for example: a window, a table, a rug, a loaf of bread, a bowl, a wine jug, etc.). Use the patterns on page 112 as a guide.
3. Cut a small towel from the terry cloth washcloth.
4. Use the permanent marker to draw lines on the stone so it looks like a loaf of bread.
5. Glue all the objects inside the box.
6. Use the diorama to tell others what happened in the upper room that night of the Passover feast.

 Prayer

Pray this prayer or a prayer of your own thanking Jesus for giving us communion to help us remember Him.

Dear Jesus,

Thank You for telling us in the Bible about remembering You when we eat and drink. Thank You that You shared the bread and the cup in the upper room that night. We also thank You, Jesus, for teaching us how to serve others. Help us, Lord, to be better at serving others and serving You. In Your name we pray.

Amen.

Upper Room

🥄 Snack Time

Bread and Juice

Ingredients: bread, grape juice

This is a perfect opportunity to teach children about Jesus sharing the bread and the cup with His disciples. Read some of the scriptures mentioned on page 110 (the upper right corner) aloud to the children. Then invite them to join in, having bread and grape juice together. Talk about what Jesus meant when He said to remember Him when we eat and drink. (You may also want to refer to 1 Corinthians 11:23–29 for more information.)

Patterns for Upper Room Diorama

Upper Room

Color and cut out the pages. Staple them in order.

The Upper Room

1

It was time to celebrate the Passover feast in the upper room. **2**

Jesus washed His disciples' feet in the upper room. **3**

Jesus knew it was His last supper with them. **4**

Jesus broke bread and shared some wine with His disciples. **5**

Remember Me.

Jesus told them, "Remember me." **6**

Name _____

U Is for Upper Room

Find and circle 5 crosses hidden in the picture.

Trace and write.

upper

114

"Serving Others" Calendar

Think about who and where you can help. You can help your friends, family, and even people you don't know. You can help at home, school, church—everywhere! Put a check in the boxes to show how you have helped today.

	Sunday	Monday	Tuesday	Wednesday	Thursday	Friday	Saturday
I helped a friend.							
I helped at home.							
I helped at school or church.							
I helped someone I didn't know.							

Voice in the Night

Hannah prayed to God for a long time for a baby. God finally answered Hannah's prayers. He gave her a son. She named him Samuel. Hannah praised God. She promised Him that she would give her child back to the Lord so he could serve the Lord for his whole life.

So when Samuel was about three years old, Hannah took him to the temple. He would live there and help Eli the priest. Eli had two sons who also lived there. But they were very wicked, and they didn't obey God.

Samuel grew older, and he learned to obey God even more. He learned how to help Eli at the tabernacle. His mother and father came to see him every year. They brought him a new robe each time they came. God was happy with Samuel.

Speak Lord, I am listening.

Eli knew that his two sons were wicked. He asked them to stop sinning, but they wouldn't listen to their father. God decided he must punish the two sons.

One night while Samuel was in bed, he heard a voice calling. He thought it was Eli. So he got up to find out what Eli wanted. Eli said, "I didn't call you." He sent Samuel back to bed. The same thing happened two more times. After the third time, Eli realized it must be the Lord talking to Samuel. He told Samuel that when it happened again he should say, "Speak Lord, I am listening."

Later that night, the Lord spoke to Samuel. He said that He was going to punish Eli's sons because of their wickedness.

After the Lord spoke this to Samuel, Samuel did not want to tell Eli what the Lord said. Eli made Samuel tell him, and Eli said, "He is God. It will be done as He sees fit."

What the Lord had spoken came true. Eli's two wicked sons soon were killed in a battle against the Philistines. Eli was sad, but he was glad that he had Samuel to help him. All of Israel recognized that Samuel was a prophet of the Lord.

Questions for Discussion

- What did Hannah pray about to God for a long time?
- What did Hannah promise to do if she had a child?
- Who did Samuel go live with?
- Who called to Samuel in the night?

Voice in the Night

 Arts and Crafts

"Listen and Obey" Speaker Phones

Materials: two, plastic drinking cups; 12-foot (3.6 m) piece of string; pen; permanent markers or stickers

Directions

1. Poke a hole in the bottom of each drinking cup with the pen.
2. Insert one end of the string through each hole, and tie a knot.
3. Decorate each cup with permanent markers or stickers.
4. Hold onto a cup and have a friend do the same with the other one.
5. Take turns speaking into the cups and listening. Say something you have learned from the Bible that God wants us to hear and remember (for example: don't lie, love others, help others, forgive someone who sins against you, pray to God and He will hear you, etc.).

 Snack Time

Samuel Small, Samuel Tall

Ingredients: cut pieces of vegetables and fruits, mini marshmallows, olives, cheese chunks, toothpicks

Provide the children with the listed ingredients. Model how to make a person using the materials above. Invite them to make a figure of Samuel as a child and then a large figure of Samuel as a grown man. The children can use the edible figures to tell the story of Samuel before they eat them.

Prayer

Pray this prayer or a prayer of your own asking God to help you listen to Him.

Dear God,

It's wonderful how You spoke to Samuel the prophet. Lord, help us listen to You like Samuel did. We know that we can listen to You by reading the Bible and doing what it tells us to do. Thank You for loving us so much and for giving us the Bible. Help us to learn from it.

Amen.

Voice in the Night

Color and cut out the pages. Staple them in order.

1

Hannah had a baby named Samuel.

2

Hannah gave Samuel back to the Lord to serve Him.

3

Samuel helped Eli the priest. Samuel was a prophet.

4

God spoke to Samuel and told him many things. Samuel was very special to God.

5

You are special to God, too!

6

V

Name _____

V Is for Voice

Color the picture.

Trace and write.

_____   _____

voice

V

Name _____

Words of Wisdom

Draw a picture of something God has taught you through His Word.

HOLY BIBLE

God speaks to me through His Word.

Woman at the Well

One day, Jesus and His disciples were walking to Galilee. On their way, they came to a town called Samaria. Jesus sat down by a well to rest. Soon a woman came along to draw water. She was a Samaritan. Jews did not like Samaritans very much. The woman also lived a very sinful life, so many townspeople didn't like her, either.

As the woman came to draw water, Jesus asked her for a drink. She said, "You are a Jew, and I am a Samaritan. How can you ask me for a drink?" The woman wondered why Jesus would talk to her because not many people liked her.

Jesus knew all about the woman and her sinful life. He wanted to help her. Jesus told her that He could give her "living water." He said ". . . *whoever drinks the water I give him will never thirst. Indeed, the water I give him will become in him a spring of water welling up to eternal life."* (John 4:14)

Jesus was talking about how He gives eternal life and how the Holy Spirit lives in people who believe in Him. Jesus then told the woman that He was the Messiah. He said He could save her from her sins. The woman believed Jesus.

After the Samaritan woman spoke with Jesus, she changed her ways. She stopped living a sinful life. She started to follow Jesus and walk in His ways. She also went back to her village to tell others about Jesus.

Many people believed in Jesus because of what the woman said and how her life was changed.

Questions for Discussion

- Why didn't many people like the woman at the well?
- What did Jesus tell the woman that He was?
- What did Jesus say He could save the woman from?
- What did the woman do after meeting Jesus?

Woman at the Well

 Arts and Crafts

"He's Changing Me" Booklet

Materials: 24" x 6" (61 cm x 15 cm) strip of paper, crayons, ribbon

Directions

1. Fold the strip of paper, accordion style, every 3" (8 cm).
2. Crease the folds.
3. In each space of the booklet, draw a picture or write a word about how you are different because of Jesus.
4. Draw or write how you show that you are living for Jesus.
5. Fold the booklet back up. Tie it with a ribbon.
6. Share the booklet with a family member or friend.

 Snack Time

Water From the Well and Popcorn

Ingredients: blue-colored juice drink (or add blue food coloring to water or milk), popcorn

Give every child a glass of the drink. As they drink their "water from the well," have them think about the story of the woman at the well.

Then pop some popcorn. Beforehand, invite the children to feel, taste, and smell the kernels. Have them notice how hard and small each kernel is. After popping the popcorn, invite the children to tell how the popcorn changed (hard to soft, not edible to edible, bland to tasty).

Then talk about how the woman at the well also changed. She went from living a sinful life to believing in and following Jesus. Invite the children to share how Jesus has changed their lives.

 Prayer

Pray this prayer or a prayer of your own asking God to help you keep your eyes on Jesus.

Dear Father in Heaven,

Help me to love Jesus more. Help me to want to follow Him in everything. Thank You that the woman at the well changed her life after she met Jesus. Help me change my ways that are wrong and follow Jesus, too.

Amen.

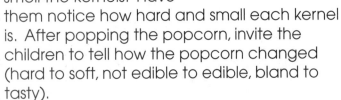

W

Woman at the Well

Color and cut out the pages. Staple them in order.

The Woman at the Well

1

Jesus asked the Samaritan woman for a drink.

2

Jesus knew this woman had sinned a lot.

3

I am the Messiah.

Jesus told the woman that he was the Messiah. She believed in Him.

4

She told everyone about the Messiah.

5

Many people believed in Jesus because of her!

6

W Is for Woman at the Well

Connect the dots to see where Jesus rested one day. Color the picture.

Trace and write.

woman

W

Name _____

Tell Others

Write this letter to a friend, telling him or her about Jesus.
Fill in the blanks, and sign your name at the bottom.

Dear _____,

Jesus is _____.
He is great because _____
_____.
I love Jesus because _____
_____.
I know Jesus loves me because
_____
_____
_____
_____.
I can tell you more about Jesus.
Just ask me.

Love,

_____

Xerxes and Esther

King Xerxes was looking for a new queen. When he saw beautiful Esther, he chose her to be his new queen. She was beautiful on the inside and out. Esther was very happy to be chosen. Esther did have a secret, however. She was Jewish!

A wicked man named Haman had a plan to kill all the Jews in the land. Esther heard about this terrible news. Since she was Jewish, she didn't want all of her family and friends to be killed. Esther didn't know what to do. Her uncle told her she'd have to go speak to the king.

But the king had some special rules. He said that people could only come and talk to him if he wanted to see them, and that included Esther. She couldn't just talk to the king any time she felt. So Esther was a little bit scared about going to talk to King Xerxes.

Esther decided to prepare a very special meal for the king. He came to the meal. He was very pleased with Esther.

Another day, Esther prepared a second very special meal for the king, which he also enjoyed. At this meal, Esther told the king about the plan of wicked Haman. Esther also told the king that she was a Jew.

The king was very angry about Haman's plan. He had Haman killed. The king was thankful to have Esther for his wife. He was proud of the courage she had in helping the Jewish people. Esther was brave, and she saved all the Jewish people in the land.

Esther was a very special woman.

Questions for Discussion

- Why did the king choose Esther as his new wife?
- What was Haman's wicked plan?
- How did Esther help the Jews?

Xerxes and Esther

 Arts and Crafts

Feast for a King

Materials: magazines, drawing paper, glue or paste, scissors, art supplies

Directions

1. Draw a large table in the center of your paper.
2. Cut pictures of food from the magazines. Paste them on the table to make a feast.
3. Draw a picture of King Xerxes at one end of the table and a picture of Queen Esther at the other end of the table.
4. Make dialogue bubbles near Queen Esther and King Xerxes.
5. Write some words inside the dialogue bubbles that might show what the king and queen may have said to each other.

 Snack Time

Dessert Fit for a King

Ingredients: chocolate sandwich cookies, peanut butter, spray whip cream, maraschino cherries

Give each child two sandwich cookies. Then have the children spread peanut butter on top of one cookie. Next, place the other cookie on top of that. Invite the children to spray whip cream on top on the cookie and top with a cherry. As the children enjoy this special dessert, invite them to talk about what Queen Esther might have served King Xerxes when she prepared the special meals for him.

 Prayer

Pray this prayer or a prayer of your own asking God to help you be brave like Esther.

Dear God,

Thank You for the story about Esther and King Xerxes. She was a very brave woman. Help us to be brave like Esther. Help us to stand up for what is right, even if we feel a little bit afraid.

Amen.

Xerxes and Esther

Color and cut out the pages. Staple them in order.

King Xerxes and Queen Esther **1**

Esther was the beautiful new queen. **2**

Haman was a wicked man. He was really mean. **3**

Haman planned to kill all Jews. Esther told the king this news. **4**

The king stopped Haman's wicked plan. **5**

Esther saved the Jews. **6**

X

Name _____

X Is for Xerxes

Use the code to color the crowns.

◇ = yellow

○ = blue

☆ = red

Trace and write.

Xerxes

X

Name _____

Storytelling Wallet

Color the picture below and cut it out on the bold line. Fold on the dashed lines and tape the short sides together. Make pictures of the story and place them in the wallet. Use it to tell the story of Esther.

Young Jesus

Jesus was born in Bethlehem to Mary and Joseph. Jesus was very special. He was the Messiah, the Christ that the Jews had been waiting for. Many people came to worship and honor Him. King Herod didn't want people to love baby Jesus more than they loved him. He was jealous of Jesus. King Herod wanted to find baby Jesus and kill him.

Mary and Joseph wanted to protect Jesus, so they left Bethlehem. They went to Egypt until King Herod died. Then they moved to Galilee in Israel.

Jesus grew up in a town called Nazareth. He lived with his mother, Mary, and her husband Joseph. Joseph was a carpenter.

Every year, Joseph and Mary went to Jerusalem to celebrate the Passover. When Jesus was twelve, He got to go along with them. When the feast of the Passover ended, Mary and Joseph began traveling home with a group of people. They thought Jesus was with them in the group. They didn't know that He stayed in Jerusalem.

After traveling for almost a day, Mary and Joseph realized that Jesus wasn't with them. They asked many friends and relatives, but no one had seen Jesus. Mary and Joseph went back to Jerusalem to find Him. They looked all over the city for Jesus, but they couldn't find Him. Three days later, they found Jesus in the temple. He was sitting among the teachers of the Law, listening carefully and asking them questions. Everyone who heard Jesus talking with the teachers were amazed at how much Jesus knew and understood about the Scriptures and about God.

When Mary and Joseph found Jesus, they were amazed. His mother said to Him, "Jesus, why did you do this to us? Your father and I have been so worried about You."

"Why were you looking for Me?" He asked. "Didn't you know that I was in My Father's house?" But they did not understand what He was saying to them. Jesus knew that God was His true Father and that the temple was His Father's house.

Then Jesus went back to Nazareth with Mary and Joseph and was obedient to them. Mary treasured all these things in her heart. Jesus grew in mind and body and in favor with God and men.

Questions for Discussion

- Why did King Herod want Jesus killed?
- After searching for three days, where did Mary and Joseph find Jesus?
- Why were the people amazed with Jesus as He sat in the temple with the teachers and priests?

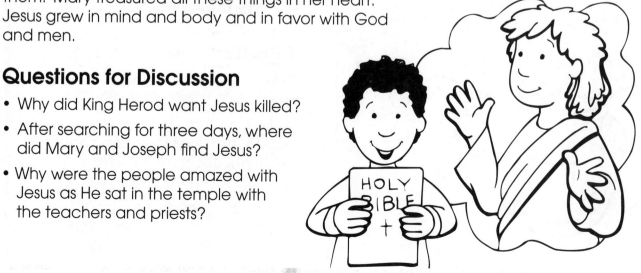

Young Jesus

 Arts and Crafts

"Young Jesus" Poster

Materials: Jesus as a boy pattern on page 133, 8" x 12" (20 cm x 30 cm) sheet of construction paper, art supplies, scissors, yarn, glue, 3" x 5" (8 cm x 13 cm) note card

Directions

1. Print **Jesus was a child, too.** across the top of the construction paper.

2. Make a copy of the Jesus as a boy pattern and glue it to the sheet of construction paper.

3. Tie several strands of yarn together to make Jesus' hair.

4. Glue the hair to Jesus' head.

5. Fold a note card and print *Holy Word* on the front.

6. Paste the "Bible" in Jesus' hand.

7. Cut a ball from the paper. Paste it in Jesus' other hand.

8. Apply stickers or use the art supplies to add a decorative border around the picture.

🥄 **Snack Time**

Yummy Yogurt

Ingredients: vanilla yogurt, fresh fruit pieces, raisins, granola

Invite the children to make this healthy snack as they talk about the things Jesus might have enjoyed when He was young.

Pour some yogurt into a bowl. Toss in several pieces of fresh fruit, raisins, and top with granola. Mix together and enjoy.

132

Young Jesus

 Prayer

Pray this prayer or a prayer of your own thanking God for sending Jesus to live on this earth.

Dear God,

Thank You for sending Jesus to live on this earth. We know Jesus is Your Son and that He is God. We also know that He experienced many of the things that we experience on the earth. Thank You that we have a Savior who knows our thoughts and feelings. Help us to go to Jesus when we are hurt or frightened or happy.

Amen.

Jesus as a Boy Pattern

Young Jesus

Color and cut out the pages. Staple them in order.

When Jesus was a young boy, He probably liked to play with friends.

1

Just like you!

2

When Jesus was a young boy, He probably liked to spend time with His family.

3

Just like you!

4

When Jesus was a young boy, He probably liked to pray to God and read God's Word.

5

Just like you!

6

Y Is for Young Jesus

Find and circle the letters hidden in this picture that spell **JESUS**.

Trace and write.

young

My Friend, Jesus

Imagine if you were one of Jesus' friends when He was a young boy. What do you think He would have been like? Draw or write about Jesus in the spaces provided.

Z Zacchaeus in a Tree

One day, Jesus was traveling through Jericho. A man named Zacchaeus, a tax collector, was in the city at the time. Zacchaeus wasn't a very honest man. Many people did not like him. When Zacchaeus heard that Jesus was coming through town, he wanted to see him. Since Zacchaeus was a very short man and couldn't see Jesus over the people in the crowds, he ran ahead of Jesus and climbed a tree. This way, he would be able to see Jesus above the crowd of people.

As Jesus came by, He looked up at Zacchaeus and said, "Zacchaeus, come down. I want to go to your house today." Zacchaeus was so happy that Jesus wanted to come to his house. He came down at once. He welcomed Jesus gladly into his home.

Many people saw this. They knew Zacchaeus was a sinner. They wondered why Jesus would want to go to his house. They began to say, "Jesus has gone to the home of a sinner."

But Zacchaeus was ready to stop sinning and to follow Jesus. He said to the Lord, "I will give half of everything I own to the poor people. I will pay back the people I have cheated. I will give them four times the amount I owe them."

Jesus was very happy about how Zacchaeus changed. *"Jesus said to him, 'Today salvation has come to this house, because this man, too, is a son of Abraham. For the Son of Man came to seek and to save what was lost.'"* (Luke 19:9–10)

The people watched as Zacchaeus started to live his life for the Lord. Jesus did many good things. He helped many people turn from their sin and follow Him.

Questions for Discussion

• Why didn't people like Zacchaeus?
• Why did Zacchaeus climb the tree?
• What happened to Zacchaeus after he met Jesus?

Z Zacchaeus in a Tree

 Arts and Crafts

My House

Materials: house pattern on page 139, sheet of light blue construction paper, several 2" x 3" (5 cm x 8 cm) white paper squares, art supplies, paste or glue, scissors, markers or crayons

Directions

1. Trace around the house pattern on the construction paper.
2. Draw a roof, chimney, trees, bushes, and flowers.
3. Make a fold on the left-hand side of each 2" x 3" white square. Then paste the edge of each square on the house so that it opens like a window.
4. Trace around each window.
5. Inside each window, draw or write about something that you would do if Jesus were coming to your house (Suggestions: pray, repent, forgive, clean my room, take a bath, bake a cake, read my Bible, etc.).

Snack Time

Cream Cheese Trees

Ingredients: cream cheese or peanut butter, celery stalks with leafy ends

Give each child a tall stalk of celery. Have the children spread cream cheese (or peanut butter) in the celery. Invite the children to stand their "trees" up as they tell how Zacchaeus climbed the tree so that he could see Jesus. Then, enjoy eating the "trees."

Prayer

Pray this prayer or a prayer of your own asking God to help you keep your eyes on Jesus.

Dear Father in Heaven,

Help me to love Jesus more. Help me to want to see Him in everything. Help me to think about Jesus many times each day. Thank You that Zacchaeus changed his life after he met Jesus. Help me change my ways that are wrong and follow Jesus, too.

Amen.

Z Zacchaeus in a Tree

House Pattern

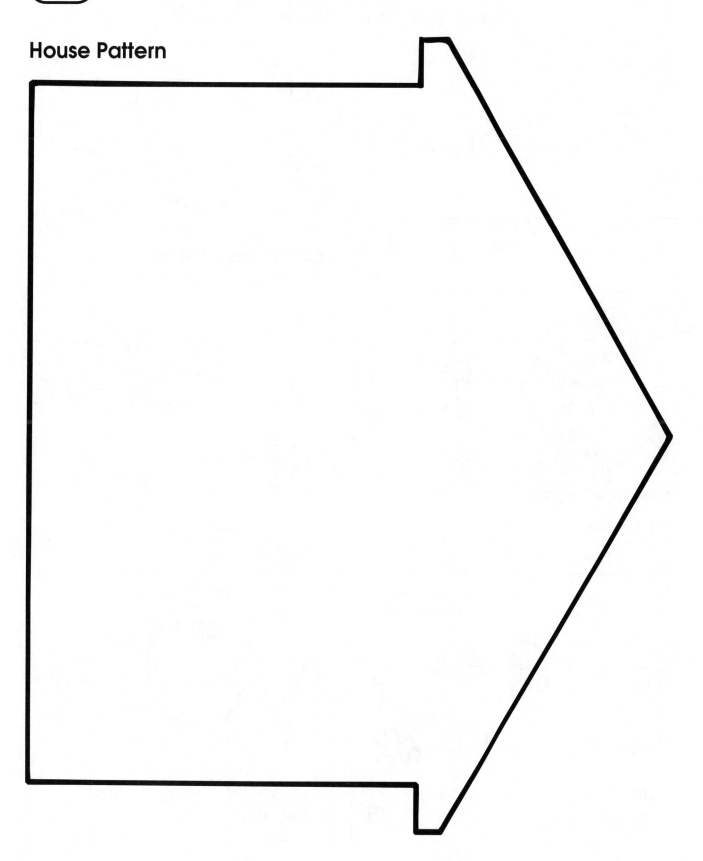

Zaccheaus

Color and cut out the pages. Staple them in order.

1

Zacchaeus climbed a tree.
Zacchaeus wanted to see. **2**

He knew that Jesus was
coming to town. **3**

Jesus told Zacchaeus to
come down. **4**

Jesus went to Zacchaeus'
house that day. **5**

Zacchaeus changed and
followed Jesus' way. **6**

Z Is for Zacchaeus

Color the picture. Count the people around the tree on the ground. Write the number on the tree trunk.

Trace and write.

Zacchaeus _____

_____

Name _____

Zacchaeus Matching Game

Color and cut apart the cards. Mix up the cards, and lay them facedown. Take turns with a friend, turning over two cards. Try to find a matching pair. When you find a pair, tell about that portion of the story.

Alphabet Quilt Recording Page

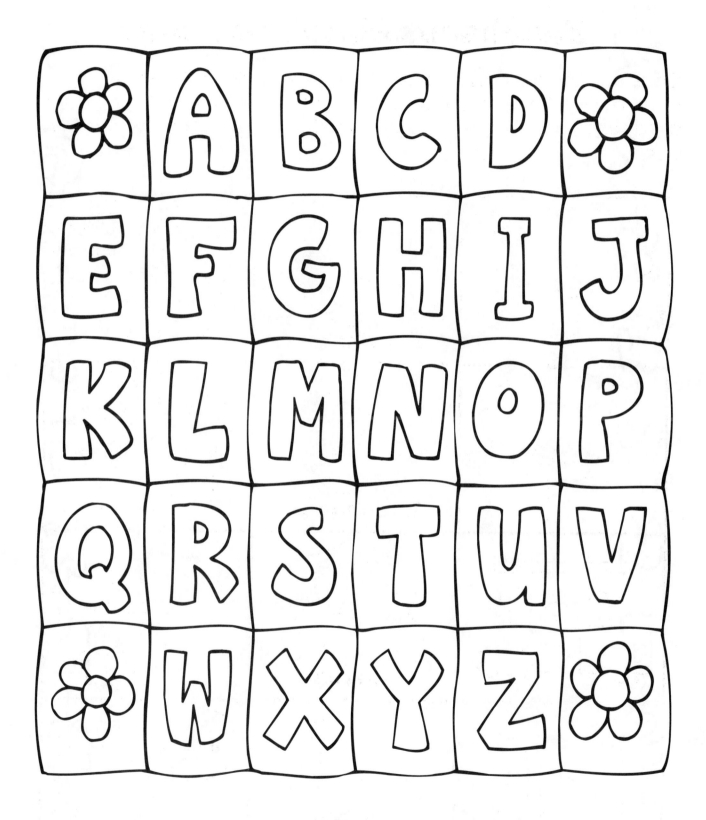